FATHER FLANAGAN'S LEGACY

Father Flanagan's Legacy:
Hope and Healing for Children

Published by the Boys Town Press
Boys Town, NE 68010

Copyright © 2003 by Father Flanagan's Boys' Home

The Boys Town Press is the publishing division of Girls and Boys Town, the original Father Flanagan's Boys' Home.

Publisher's Cataloging in Publication

Father Flanagan's legacy : hope and healing for children / editors: Barbara A. Lonnborg and Thomas J. Lynch. -- Boys Town, NE : Boys Town Press, 2003.

    p. ; cm.
    ISBN-13: 978-1-889322-56-8 (pbk.)
    ISBN-10: 1-889322-56-3 (pbk.)

    1. Flanagan, Edward Joseph, 1886-1948. 2. Father Flanagan's Boys' Home. 3. Problem children--Institutional care--United States. 4. Problem children--Behavior modification--United States. 5. Social work--United States--Biography. I. Lonnborg, Barbara A. II. Lynch, Thomas J. III. Title.

HV876 .F38 2003
362.70973--dc21   0306

10 9 8 7 6 5 4 3 2

Father Flanagan's Legacy

Hope and Healing for Children

EDITORS

BARBARA A. LONNBORG AND THOMAS J. LYNCH

BOYS TOWN, NEBRASKA

Also from the Boys Town Press

For a free Boys Town Press catalog, call 1-800-282-6657
Visit our Web site at www.boystownpress.org

TABLE OF CONTENTS

Memories of Father Flanagan

In 2003, Bill Talbod was the oldest living alumnus of Father Flanagan's Boys' Home.

⋈⋈

MY MOTHER PASSED AWAY WHEN I WAS EIGHT, and my family began to break up. I lived in Kansas City, Missouri, and would often run away from home and bum around on the streets. The police would pick me up and take me back home. My father had heard about Father Edward Flanagan's Boys' Home in Omaha, Nebraska, and he had my older sister bring me there in February of 1920.

After living at the Home for several months, I went to live with a farm family in Minnesota. I became very lonesome for my family and Father Flanagan's Home, so I ran away and hid at a schoolhouse for several days. I became so hungry, I stole a chicken and sold it for a dollar to buy food. Realizing I could not continue to live without a home, I walked fifteen miles to a nearby town and sought out the local priest. I told him my story, and that I wanted to return to Father Flanagan's Home.

A local businessman agreed to drive me from Minnesota back to Father Flanagan and what was then called the old German[-American] home. As I rode up 13th Street to the Home, I could see the Sisters gathered on the steps waiting for me to come "home." They said Father Flanagan wanted to see me, so I went to his office. After telling him all my troubles, including stealing the chicken, he came over and gave me a hug, and said, "You did the right thing, and I welcome you home."

That memory has stayed with me my whole life.

I have often thought of Father Flanagan starting out in the old house in downtown Omaha with a few kids from the municipal courts. It just kept growing. The boys I lived with were from disrupted homes, and not bad boys. Father Flanagan was good to all the boys and treated them the same regardless of race or religion.

It was tough times for Father Flanagan raising money to feed all of us because the Home kept growing. I remember Father attempting to raise money to purchase Overlook Farm and give the boys a permanent home of their own. Even in all the tough times, Father Flanagan was always kind to the boys. He was not kind to those who tried to discipline the boys. He would say, "If there's any punishment to take place, I will do it myself."

After I left the Home, I fought in World War II as a technical sergeant with General George Patton in North Africa. I was wounded in the invasion of North Africa and was forced to retire early. The years after the war were hard for me, but the lessons I had learned at Boys Town stayed with me and helped me survive.

I have talked to all the schools here in Worthington, Minnesota, about my life and the importance of Boys Town. I tell them the lessons I learned from Father Flanagan: to think of yourself as somebody, to know you can succeed and be a leader. To the children of Girls and Boys Town today, I tell them to have faith, and that it is very easy to live a good life.

If my father had not sent me to Father Flanagan and Boys Town, my life would have gone haywire. I have lived a good life.

Father Flanagan's Boys' Home is a place that I will never forget.

– BILL TALBOD
Worthington, Minnesota, 2003
Boys Town Resident, 1920

CHAPTER ONE

Boys Town, City of Little Men

In 1917, an Irish immigrant priest, Father Edward J. Flanagan, was running a shelter for homeless and out-of-work men in downtown Omaha, and he was discouraged. For, no matter how many men he fed or found jobs for, so many remained helpless and hopeless of ever turning their lives around. Out of that despair, however, grew a conviction that if lives and souls were to be saved, the work needed to start at the beginning, not the middle or end, of life.

By the end of that year, Father Flanagan had embarked on a life's mission that would bring hope for a better life to thousands of young boys who faced poverty, neglect, homelessness, or even incarceration. From the start, his Home for Boys was racially inclusive, nonsectarian, and committed to love and rehabilitation rather than punishment – attitudes that were remarkably forward thinking for the times. Thirty years later, Father Flanagan was globally admired as a champion of children and dozens of other homes for boys were operating around the world in emulation of his work.

In the following essay, he describes the origin of the Home and the reasons for his methods of child care.

⚹⚹

WITH A BORROWED $90 AND FIVE BOYS, two from the juvenile court and three homeless, I created and founded my first home for boys in December, 1917. More than five thousand homeless, abandoned and neglected boys have called Boys Town their home in the twenty-eight years that have followed.

Boys Town is a monument to the men and women who, through their cooperation and financial support, have evidenced their belief that there is no such thing as a bad boy; who believe that the homeless and neglected boy can be taken from the streets, from the reform school, from bad environment, and be molded into useful American citizens.

Prior to my venture with a home for boys, I worked with men whose circumstances were unfortunate. My idea was to do something tangible for the down-and-outers I had come to know so well in my voluntary visits to the city jail.

This work, however, was not deemed successful. Although some good had been accomplished, I decided I had the cart before the horse, and so reversed the procedure and began with boys, still in their formative years.

An analysis of some two thousand case histories of unfortunate men, pieced together from little confidences freely offered, showed the vast majority of these drifters were mired in the gutters because of a neglected, homeless childhood.

By Edward J. Flanagan, 1945 article, from the Girls and Boys Town Hall of History archives.

The first home for boys was an old, ten-room house near the business section of Omaha, Nebraska. Enrollment soon increased. Large facilities were needed. Resources were meager in those early days of the home. But there was faith and hope. I knew the support and generosity of the American people would never let this program down. And in some way, bills were met and progress was made in those trying days of the twenties.

The first buildings at Boys Town were temporary frame, barrack-type buildings. They were modest, indeed, in comparison with those to be found here today, but to the boys the home and the school were the best in the country.

Boys Town is not by any stretch of the imagination an orphanage. It is a complete community in itself – the smallest incorporated city in the country – with its own first-class post office, its own grade and high school, trade school, print shop, gymnasium, church, movie theatre, swimming pool, farm, infirmary, athletic field, dining hall, and apartments.

… I always have favored self-government for my boys. Boys will develop into better American citizens if they have their own government. Because of this belief, the Douglas County board of commissioners was asked to make Boys Town an incorporated village, and this was done in 1936. So today Boys Town is actually an incorporated village – "A City of Little Men."

City officials are elected by and from the boys at semi-annual elections. The young citizens take their elections seriously. I have watched people vote in various city, state and national elections; but never have I seen voters take more seriously their privilege and responsibility of voting than do the citizens of Boys Town.

The training in operating the government of Boys Town teaches each boy to be better citizens later in life. It shows each boy the difference between good government and bad government.

For a week before each election, the campus truly is a political hotbed. There is the usual number of political signs and political rallies.

Don't think for a moment that these city officials are mere figureheads. They have their duties to perform just as do the city officials of any city. And they fulfill their duties well. It is an honor with them to serve Boys Town, and each commissioner wants to do his job well.

In addition to his other official duties, the mayor is the official greeter. If a movie star or some other celebrity comes to Boys Town, it is the duty of the mayor to be on the reception committee and escort the visitor around the grounds.

Each apartment building has its own court. After hearing the cases, the Boys Town judge decides the fate of the offenders. Penalties are restricted privileges and added duties.

Our high school offers courses in civics and problems of American democracy, both of which are intended to help make a better citizen and a better informed citizen.

I believe that the training a boy gets in practical government is sounder training than the theories advanced in the classroom, although both are important and receive their proper recognition. But there is nothing like practical experience such as our boys get in managing their own government.

Our school is accredited by the State of Nebraska and is, I believe, one of the finest that can be found anywhere in a community of like size. Our teachers are chosen because of their outstanding ability and training and because of their proven success in working with boys.

Boys Town has a band, an orchestra and a choir of one hundred voices which are nationally known as the result of their many performances over the radio. Membership in all groups is voluntary.

A boy also must have a strong body. Our recreational program is directed by a full-time athletic director. Every boy is enrolled in the physical education program. Our high school boys represent Boys Town in track, baseball, basketball and football. We also have an intra-mural program for other boys in all seasonal sports.

Boys are kept actively engaged throughout the day. There are an assorted number of leisure time and hobby activities. Such groups include 4-H club activities, stamp collecting, a camera club, model plane construction, leathercraft and woodwork.

Every boy has his particular chore to perform, his school work, religious training, recreational period and leisure time activities to help round out each day's schedule.

I believe the best insurance for the future of America and of the American way of living lies in the adequate healthy care of our American youth. Upon the training of today's children rests the future of the American system.

My aim is to give still fuller meaning to that concept of America as a land of opportunity – opportunity for the neglected and unfortunate boy as well as for the boy who has all the blessed advantages of loving parents, good home and adequate schooling.

I have said, and I say again and again, that there is no such thing as a bad boy. There is only bad environment, bad training, bad example, bad thinking. The child comes unspoiled from the hands of God. Understanding and not punishment is the solution for what commonly is called "juvenile delinquency." This is not just a statement. It is verified by more than a quarter of a century of work with boys of all classes.

A boy is not a static creature. He is a growing individual, a bundle of possibilities, seeking expression and development in a thousand and one ways. What kind of a citizen he becomes depends upon what kind of training and guidance he is given. This is the inherent right of every boy – not of the privileged boy only – that he shall have a good home, pleasant environment and the opportunity to become a useful citizen through adequate training and normal associations.

Each year Boys Town graduates go out from our high school to take their place in the community as useful citizens. They are to be found all over the land, busy at work, carrying their full share of responsibility as members of their communities, enjoying the happiness of their own home and family.

And nowhere is there to be found a greater sense of appreciation than in the heart of the child. They so want to please. Sometimes they are a bit self-conscious and incoherent in verbal expressions of appreciation, but the eloquence of their acts and ambitions would soften the heart of the most confirmed skeptic.

One of the deepest joys I have is reading the hundreds of letters which my former boys write. I wish you might read some of them. You would say that no dollar was ever better invested than that which is given for the good of some boy. No other investment pays greater dividends. We cannot, we must not, we will not let these homeless and neglected youth down.

 # LOVE AND DUTY

If a few short words could sum up the essence of Father Flanagan, those words might be: love of God, love of neighbor, and devotion to duty. In a series of "Little Talks to Children," published in 1930 editions of Father Flanagan's Boys' Home Journal, he explained his heartfelt conviction that these traits were essential to building the character of young people. Excerpts from these talks follow.

✻✻

Love of God set Edward Flanagan on the course early in life of joining the priesthood. As a young seminarian in New York, he volunteered to visit patients in hospital tuberculosis wards, and soon was battling his own bout of pneumonia. Sent home from seminaries in both New York and Rome due to his frail health, he persevered and finally found, in the dry mountain air of Innsbruck, Austria, the climate that allowed him to complete his studies and be ordained.

I SAY, MY DEAR LITTLE FRIENDS, that you are the children of God. He created you for Himself, so that you may eternally glorify Him in Heaven. He loves you more than anyone in this world. He created you, gave you life, health, happiness, beautiful bodies, wonderful minds, and placed in you an immortal soul, which is a likeness of Himself. Everything that is good in life comes from Him, and is given to you that you may enrich yourselves for Eternity in heaven with Him.

These many acts of love on His part should be sufficient reason for you to love Him always in return, and never do anything that might offend Him. Yet, my dear children, even our first parents Adam and Eve sinned against this great Friend, and as a consequence so deeply wounded His Divine Heart that He dismissed them and their future children, the human race, forever from living in Paradise with Him. The infinite love of God, however, relented, and saved man from this edict. He sent His Divine and Only Son to earth to atone for this ingratitude of the sins of man. This "God made Man" came to earth to live with the children of men and to teach them by word and example His new Commandment of Love; and finally to fully propitiate for man's offenses, this Innocent Lamb of God offered Himself as a victim to an ignominious death on the Cross of Calvary. "Greater love than this," my dear children, "no man hath, than that he lay down his life for his friend."

What makes this love even greater is the fact that God is omnipotent and all-sufficient in Himself. He did not need you or me. He did not need the world. It was entirely out of an overflowing Heart of Love that he created us, and to share with us some of His great happiness. He has created us to make us happy. When by sin we lost this chance to happiness, He took upon Himself the burden of our guilt, and like the Good Shepherd which He is, brought us back to the fold, and gave us another chance.

Now my dear children, this great Lover of ours – this great Master and Father does not make it difficult for us to attain the happiness for which He has created us. He loves us entirely too much to make Eternal Life difficult to obtain. The truth is, He has given but Ten Laws which he asks us to follow and obey so that we may make ourselves worthy of Eternity in Heaven with Him. He has asked us to conform our lives to the Ten Commandments, and by doing so give Him some evidence that we love Him in return for the great love that He is constantly bestowing upon us.

Would not it be terrible, my dear children, to hurt Him Who loves us so infinitely much? You would not slap your father or mother, would you? Of course not! They are so near and dear to you, and have done so much for you that you would consider it a most terrible thing ever to pain them. Yet, this is exactly what we do to the Great Father, Who has given us our parents, and Who has done infinitely more for us than they have! When we violate His Commandments, we slap Him in the face; in spite of all His great love, we rebel against Him, and say that we do not want His love.

There is only one excuse that we can ever give for violating God's Commandments and that is that we do not love Him at all. When we sin we openly tell our God that we love ourselves and our sinful desires far more than we do the Innocent Lamb of Calvary Who died to save us for Eternity. ...

This is sin and its effects, my dear children, and I am certain that thus knowing and understanding its heinousness, none of you would willfully and intentionally commit one by violating the Ten Commandments of God.

><:><

Love of his neighbor defined Father Flanagan's life as a priest. Seeking to do more than routine parish work, he first opened a "Workingmen's Hotel" for men out of work and down on their luck. He spent the final thirty-one years of his life defeating drought, depression, prejudice, and ignorance in order to provide a home for abandoned and neglected boys. Service to others was deeply ingrained in his character. "Christian charity," he once said, "does not consist in the shedding of tears, or in mere preaching, but rather in the doing of that which we preach, and in the actual alleviation of the conditions that bring about those tears."

... LAST MONTH I POINTED OUT to you the greatest of all reasons for keeping the Commandments, and this reason was Love – Love for the great God of Love.

Do you know, my dear children, that these Ten Laws of God may be even more simplified, and may be fully expressed in two main precepts which are: "Thou shalt love the Lord thy God with thy whole heart and thy whole soul, and with thy whole strength. This is the greatest and the first commandment. And the second," which is inseparable from the first, is: "Thou shalt love thy neighbor as thyself." ...

Why should we love our neighbors as ourselves? First of all, my dear little friends, because we are all children of the same Father, and of the same large family – the human race. Rich and poor, great and small, Christians and infidel, Protestants and Jews, Gentiles and Catholics; we all have our origin from God, and we are all destined for God. This is the reason why we naturally love one another when we are not influenced by selfishness and passion.

Unfortunately, however, man's selfishness has caused him to forget his neighbor and often to despise and hate him. How unnatural this is, my dear children, and how harmful? It is this absence of love among ourselves that is responsible for much of the misery and suffering of the world. Without love for each other, there is no sympathy, no pity, no mercy. We become ferocious beasts of the jungle, always seeking to hurt one another.

What a peaceful and happy society we would live in, if we would only love one another. Most of the suffering and poverty with which the world is afflicted would be eliminated. The rich and the healthy would be compassionate with the poor and the sick; they would visit them in their hovels and would alleviate their hunger and their suffering. The poor in return would be more considerate of the rich, and would do everything in their power to help and aid them.

But as it is today, we have forgotten that we are all children of the same family, and that we all come from the same source and are destined to the same end. As a consequence, the world must live in discord until we again love our neighbor as Christ has loved us.

This brings us to the second great reason for loving one another, and that consists in the examples set by our Master, Jesus Christ. We are all brothers in Jesus Christ, and members of his mystic body. As the parts of our physical body respond to each other's needs, and cooperate in all actions, so should we also as parts of the Mystic Body of Christ, sympathize with the miseries of one another; assist one another in our needs; and love one another with the most sincere of loves. We should follow the examples given us by our great model, Jesus Christ. His whole earthly life was spent in one continual act of love for fellow-man. Both in His hidden and public life, His every word and action was prompted by the most tender charity for suffering mankind. ...

[C]an we pretend to be His followers if we do not even love man to the extent of attempting to aid and encourage him, and to alleviate his sufferings when that is within our power? ...

Often during His lifetime, Jesus reminded His disciples of this commandment, but lest they forget it, He returns again to it on the eve of His Death, and says: "My children, my little children, I am going to leave you. But before I separate Myself from you, I wish to give you a New Commandment, which is to love one another as I have loved you."

This is the love, my dear children, with which we must permeate all our actions with our fellow-man. ... We must not let hatred and revenge have a place in our lives. They are unworthy of a Christian. We must not let unjust dealings be known among us, for Christ, our Master, taught a different Gospel. If our brother is sick and in need, we must visit him and help him; if he is hungry, we must feed him; if he is thirsty, we must give him drink; if he is naked, we must clothe him; if he is homeless, we must harbor him; if he is lonely and unfortunate, we must open our hearts to him.

This, my dear children, is the second greatest of Commandments, and as Christ said, "This is My Commandment."

✠✠

Good habits, work, discipline, and responsibility were also cherished bywords of Father Flanagan. "It is a work-a-day world into which our youngsters are born, and there will always be work to do. The keenest satisfaction they will ever achieve will come from tasks well accomplished, obstacles overcome, and goals achieved," he said.

IN ORDER THAT WE MAY GROW UP into honest and virtuous men and women, we should early in life begin the formation of good habits. As we train ourselves in childhood, so we will be when we develop into maturity. If as children we repeatedly allow ourselves to tell lies and to steal things, then we can depend upon it that as grown up people lying and stealing will have become such a habit with us that they can be uprooted only with the greatest difficulty.

A habit, my dear children, is nothing else than the result of repeated acts, whether they be good or bad. After doing a certain thing time and time again, our will becomes subject to that action, and we get so that eventually we do it whether we wish to or not. For instance, a child that has trained himself to always tell the truth, regardless of the circumstances or results, will eventually acquire the habit of truthfulness, and the virtue will become so firmly a part of him that no temptations of loss or gain could compel him ever to swerve from the truth. On the other hand, a child who tells lies frequently, acquires that habit and becomes a slave to it, and later in life will become just a common liar. This holds true of all the virtues and vices. We acquire these virtues and vices in childhood, and then by the repeated practice of them, form habits that will determine our character as mature men and women. When, then, your parents or teachers correct you for your faults they do so in order to save you from developing bad habits that would ruin your future.

It is just as easy, my dear children, to form good habits as it is to form bad ones. You are now going through that period of life in which this formation takes place, and it would be well for you to check up on your daily acts, to find out just what kind of habits you are forming. Are they good, or indifferent? If you are really interested in becoming successful men and women, you will at once check the formation of those habits which are bad, and will be most anxious to strive to acquire those that will result in the building up of true Christian character.

Now how can this be accomplished? I might answer in a brief and general way: "It is accomplished by doing our daily duty." This means that we must do everything that we ought to do, and includes our obligations toward God, toward our neighbors and toward ourselves. What these obligations are you already know from my previous talks to you. They are comprised in the Ten Commandments of God, and consequently, when we form the habit of abiding by these Commandments, we have done our duty to all.

Let me impress upon your minds, that it is not sufficient to know our duties, or to perform them when we wish or spasmodically; we must practice them at all times, regardless of the temptations that may be incentives to do otherwise. To do our duty occasionally or "by fits and starts" helps us but little on the way of life. A dutiful and virtuous man is no more built by stray acts of duty, than is a house built by loose stones scattered all over the field. Until the doing of our duty becomes a necessity with us, we cannot say that we have formed its habits. It must be so firmly imbedded in our characters that we cannot do otherwise.

The first duty that you children have is one toward your parents, who are your first and most important teachers, and who are held responsible by God for your characters. It is your duty to love and respect them, and to obey their every wish. It is your duty to be guided by their teachings and examples, and never to complain if they check your bad habits or faults. Their whole interest in life is to develop in you good and religious habits that will make you successful ..., a credit to them and a glory to Almighty God.

Sometimes, my dear children, it is not easy and pleasant to do the things that will eventually result in good habits. At first it may be very difficult to tell the truth, to always obey your parents, to go to church, to study at the appointed time, and to always do the things that we should do. But we must set our minds on the particular habit that we wish to form, and then without fail do the particular act required; eventually we will do it unconsciously and automatically, and it will become a great pleasure for us because we have gained a victory.

And now, my dear children, and you boys in particular, who find it hard to do your duty, and who occasionally get into trouble, because you try to do everything but it, think this matter over seriously. Are you happy in avoiding your duty? Of course you are not. Neither are your parents and friends who are interested in you. You have occasionally tried to do your duty, haven't you? And doing it made you happy. Now if you try and form the habit of doing your duty at all times, even though you will find it hard, at first, you will be surprised what a change will come over you when the habit of duty will be formed. And never forget, my dear children, that you depend for everything, on God. He will help you, if you only ask Him, and with this assistance and your own earnest efforts, you cannot help but succeed in forming the habit of duty toward God, your neighbors, and yourself.

CHAPTER THREE

 # EARLY DAYS IN THE HOME

Although Father Flanagan had received permission from the archbishop to open his Home for Boys in 1917, the Home received no money from the diocese for its operation. So to make ends meet, Flanagan appealed to local businesses, farmers, and women's clubs for food, furniture, and clothing. Sometimes, he literally worried where the next meal would come from. In their book, "Father Flanagan of Boys Town," authors Fulton Oursler and Will Oursler described those hard-scrabble early days when the Home survived on hand-me-downs and answered prayers.

⊁⊰

AT THE START THERE WERE FIVE BOYS. ... Of the beginning five, three were homeless orphans paroled to Flanagan a few days before and two had been assigned to his care by the juvenile court on that very morning of December 12, 1917.

He brought the first two over from the court in the morning and hustled together the other three later in the afternoon.

At the door of the new home to greet the arrivals were all the members of his staff – two nuns and a novice of the School Sisters of Notre Dame "lent" to the home by Archbishop [Jeremiah] Harty.

In the entrance hall the first two boys who arrived looked around with incredulous eyes, and the older one remarked: "We're gonna be living in a swell dump!"

Swell it did seem to their unaccustomed eyes. Alas, it was, in fact, no gleaming mansion. The founder had only a few weeks to gather the furnishings. He and his brothers, sisters, and friends had launched an intensive door-to-door campaign begging for old furniture.

The result was a weird conglomeration of attic castoffs. Nothing matched anything else. The chairs around the dining-room table represented a half dozen ages and designs in furniture making, a broken-down Duncan Phyfe forgery to a Macy basement special. The meager supply of chinaware, the knives and forks and spoons formed a rag bag, a junk box of kitchen equipment. So, too, on the second floor; a chaotic jumble of beds, cots, blankets, and spreads brought into orderly usefulness in the dormitories. ...

Such was the start of Father Flanagan's Home for Boys – a hastily furnished potpourri of secondhand things. His five first boarders reacted well for boys eight to ten years old. Once they had met the Sisters and deposited their few belongings on their beds, they set out to explore, from cellar to attic. By dinnertime they were over much of their strangeness, so that the Sisters had to yank two of them apart; hostilities had started over who was to have the bed by the window.

During the meal they plied Father Flanagan with questions. Were other boys coming in? Would they be going to school? Would they have time for play outside? He was frank with them:

"I don't know everything yet, you see. But there'll be school, sure. And there'll be time for play, too. Outside, if it's good weather. But you've got to stay out of the street now."

Not that any of these first five boys had committed crimes. Their worst offense lay in having no homes. The two who had been turned over to him by the juvenile court that morning were brothers. Many years later, during the Second World War, one of these brothers wrote back to Father Flanagan from the Southwest Pacific:

"That morning in December of 1917 is indelibly stamped into my brain. I can never forget how, after the juvenile authorities had relinquished my brother and I and we were in your custody, you presented me with a bag of chocolates and I felt pretty good about it even then.

"When we got to your home on Twenty-fifth and Dodge and you had introduced us to Sister Rose, who then showed us our room, I remember how you had to rush away without even so much as a bite to eat.

"Every time I eat spaghetti I think of the Italian kid. Remember his mother used to bring us a quart of spaghetti every Sunday which was looked upon as a great delicacy to us in those days? As far as that goes, it would be quite delicious right now."

Father talked to them as if they were grownups.

"We've all got a lot of things to do – and to learn. We've got to get a school started here. And we've got somehow to get new clothes for you all, too."

His tone always revealed a slight touch of panic and bewilderment as he took stock of his tasks. Many a skeptic, listening to him, would take him for an impractical fellow – only to find he was up against an invincible man who prayed to God all day long!

Very soon he was reminded anew by his empty pockets how short he was of funds, how he was existing on a day-to-day basis. The gifts came in slowly, hardly enough to pay for the food they needed. And the amount of food they needed increased daily as more and more boys were sent into the home by admiring judges who, however, had no way to appropriate cash for the job they cheered him for doing.

There was, too, a vast difference between running a hotel for tramps and a home for boys. He was no longer an innkeeper for weary men; he was father and mother now for a houseful of exuberant boys – he was head of a home!

Soon Father Flanagan was torn between two great efforts. One was the job of sending out begging letters; the other to organize the program of work and play.

A few nights after the home opened he woke up to hear one of the boys crying. He got up and stalked into the room to find the boy sitting up in bed. He had an earache. Now that was something new to Father Flanagan. What ought he to do? Call in a doctor?

"When I used to have an earache," another boy volunteered in a matter-of-fact tone, "my mother always used to hoist me up and carry me around and sing."

The priest in his nightgown pondered the problem dolefully. Then he lifted up the boy and began to pace up and down the room, humming a tune softly, from old memories of his mother and her lullaby in Roscommon. In a little while the child was asleep, and Flanagan felt immensely proud of the therapeutic qualities of voice.

><:><

His five young charges did their best to help, although they were more nuisance than assistance. One had dreams of being a juggler and wanted to see how many plates he could stack in one hand. After a downfall of china, his juggling lessons were restricted to pie plates, after hours.

Before the end of the first week, before Father Flanagan had got fairly under way, there were fifteen in the home. Every bed and cot was occupied and he must get more right away – and that took time.

In his crisis, fortunately, word came from Archbishop Harty that he was now satisfied the new work was so important that he was relieving Father of all pastoral duties. The message came none too soon.

"It seems to me that every time I turn around," he told Sister Rose with a lugubrious shake of the head, "there is another poor boy arriving from juvenile court. Even I never realized until now there were so terribly many homeless boys."

By Christmas Eve, less than two weeks after he had opened the doors, there were twenty-five boys in the home. The entire second floor of the house was given over to cots and beds.

><:><

Already they represented a variety of race and religion –
Catholic, Protestant, and Jew, brown, white, yellow. From the
first there was no segregation of any kind. Color or race never
made any difference to Father Flanagan, and the sole religious
requirement was that each boy attend services regularly in the
church of his own faith. Run by a Catholic priest, and with the
aid of Catholic nuns, the home began as, and has ever since
remained, a non-sectarian shelter for the homeless.

But with all his good intentions, Father Flanagan's boys did
not become angels overnight.

Perhaps things had gone along too evenly during the first
week. In the second week, as the home began to become
crowded, the headache of running a houseful of squirming,
shouting boys began to be manifest.

It might start at dark with a scream from the second floor –
a cry so loud and piercing that Father Flanagan and the Sisters
would leap from their beds to see what was wrong. They never
knew what they were going to find, a fight in the middle of the
night or a new boy scared by a nightmare.

At dawn it might begin with an early riser, playing fireman.
One tore the sheet from his bed, tied it to the bedpost, and
threw the other end out of the window. By the time Father
Flanagan had arrived, the culprit had climbed out the window
and started down his "fire escape." Halfway down he got scared
and screamed. Hardly had he rescued the boy when there was
another commotion on the main floor. Five boys, helping to
clean the living room, had got into an argument and in the
melee smashed the best living-room chair. Meanwhile the front
doorbell was ringing. Two more boys from juvenile court.

Like so many other things in this world, the beginning was the hardest. The warmth in Flanagan's heart did not chill, even though – while trying to get organized – a lot of time was needed to keep the little darlings from tearing down the place.

"Jimmy stole my sweater."

"The other boys are picking on me."

"Father, two of the boys have taken my best and only frying pan and are using it for a drum out in the back yard."

Sometimes, for an hour or so, he would steal away to the house where his parents and brothers and sisters were living. And as they listened to his doleful stories, he found himself laughing as he talked:

"They're wonderful, you know. And it's going to be much better when we get it all straightened out. But sometimes the things they do – it's hard to understand why they do them, you know."

His mother would smile at her son.

"And what did you expect, Father Edward?" she would say. "When you were a boy, you would do some queer things yourself."

He could not remember anything comparable in his own boyhood. But he would start back, reminding himself over and over that patience was one of the great lessons of life, only to learn from the Sisters what had happened while he was gone.

Perhaps that was the day Tommy and Len had fought with scissors. Or when several of the boys had borrowed one of the few tablecloths to play ghost in the basement. Someone – identity unknown – having left the tap open, the bathtub had overflowed and the water was dripping down from the kitchen ceiling.

Fresh excitement upstairs. Young voices calling down to him, "Father! Quick!"

In quavering excitement, they told him it was about Danny. What about him? Danny had vanished!

That was tough! The reason Danny was in the home was because he had run away repeatedly. Brought up by a sickly mother and a father who bullied him, the boy had become nervous and easily upset. Away from his family, even in these few days, he had seemed to improve.

The search began. It covered the entire house, upstairs and down, the grounds and blocks around. Danny's clothes were still there and his few other belongings. But no sign of Danny.

In the shadows of the hall on the second floor there was a closet. As he walked past this, Father Flanagan thought he heard a noise. It sounded like stifled laughter. He turned quickly and opened the closet door.

There was Danny, seated on the floor, laughing uproariously. With a sigh, Father Flanagan left Danny to the admonishments of the Sisters and went down to his office where bills for the week's food were piled up.

⋈⋈

Christmas was only a day away when he and the Sisters took counsel together on what they could serve for the holiday dinner.

"We have hardly enough left for just an ordinary meal," Sister Rose lamented. "Unless that lady sends over some more spaghetti, like she did last week, I don't know ----"

The doorbell interrupted. This time it was not a new boy, but a delivery man with a barrel, all bound around with a red Christmas ribbon from which dangled a card. Hope revived; someone had sent them a kilderkin of Christmas joy. Out into the kitchen they rolled it, and knocked off the top. What was inside? Sauerkraut!

That Christmas party was unique. No gifts! No tree! But the boys strung up some homemade decorations, and they all sang carols. In the morning, Mass in the tiny chapel; while boys of Protestant background went outside to worship in their own faith.

And later, Christmas dinner: for twenty-five famished boys, plates piled high with the main course – sauerkraut.

"I wish it were something else, boys – dear," Father said from the head of the table. "But it isn't, so we'll be grateful for what we have. And may Almighty God look down mercifully this day and every day on all homeless wanderers!"

They all plunged into the sauerkraut and for a while there was silence. Then a boy who had finished held up his plate: "Father – can I have some more turkey? One plate lasts awful quick!"

There was a small giggle somewhere and then yells of laughter. Contentedly Father Flanagan started in on his own second helping of sauerkraut, no longer any panic in his bosom. The warmth around the table was his answer. Praise God for the resilience and elasticity and native humor of the forsaken lads! They could take it!

He closed his eyes and let the organ music from the Apocalypse of St. John the Divine roll through his whole being:

And God shall wipe away all tears from their eyes:
And death shall be no more,
Nor mourning, nor crying, nor sorrow shall be any more,
For the former things are passed away.

He forgot the bills and other harassments. The job could be done. Things were all right. They would all come through with colors flying – the boys and their home.

CHAPTER FOUR

 # A Message of Tolerance

"I see no disaster threatening us because of any particular race, creed or color," Father Flanagan once wrote. *"But I do see danger for all in an ideology which discriminates against anyone politically or economically because he or she was born into the 'wrong' race, has skin of the 'wrong' color, or worships at the 'wrong' altar."*

FROM THE BEGINNING, HIS BOYS' HOME not only welcomed children of all races and religions, but treated them equally as well. Four years after the home's founding, Father Flanagan purchased Overlook Farm, then ten miles distant from Omaha, and moved his boys to the relatively secluded acres – at least partially to escape the criticism and uneasiness of his city neighbors with his unorthodox methods of raising children.

Oscar Flakes, one of the first African-American boys at the home, remembered the tolerance encouraged among the boys: "We all slept together, ate together, played together, and fought together and everything. We were just ordinary kids."

But living on the farm didn't isolate the boys completely from experiencing the sting of ignorance and prejudice. Flakes was a member of the "World's Greatest Juvenile Entertainers," a troupe of boys put together by Flanagan in the 1920s to travel the Midwest, first by circus wagon and then by train, entertaining small town audiences with songs, skits, jokes, and speeches.

"I like to think of music as being the language of the soul," said Flanagan. "It reveals to us truth and beauty beyond the power of words to describe. Music goes beyond the barriers of race, creed, or geography. It is a spiritual medium of mutual fellowship for all people – for the rich and the poor, for the mighty and the meek, for the old and for the young."

Flanagan's love of music and his belief in its healing powers led to the formation first of the Juvenile Entertainers and later a full-size band and choir. Away from the farm and on the road, the troupes performed, spreading word of the boys' home and seeking donations to keep it running. In some places, town folk had never seen a racially mixed group.

"We went into [towns] where they hadn't even seen a colored person," according to Flakes. "In Beatrice, Nebraska, there were no colored at that time. When we gave a performance at night, sometimes people would come up – people were very poor then and some of them couldn't afford money, so they would take us and board us and feed us for overnight. This little girl came up on the stage and would look at me. I know she was very small and very young compared to what we were. She would walk around me and go back to her mother. Finally, she brought her mother over, and she said (they were picking the kids they would like to stay overnight), 'Mother, take him home and wash his face so that he will be clean like me.' I remember that."

Wherever the boys traveled, Flanagan insisted that all the boys be treated as they were at the home. At times, the troupe, and later the band, choir, and sports teams, would have invitations rescinded when it was learned the groups were integrated. One minister, a member of the Ku Klux Klan, threatened to tar and feather the group if it performed in his community.

But, sometimes, Father Flanagan's message of tolerance made an impression. Flakes remembered an incident that took place in South Dakota:

"Seven of us boys were there. We had come in in the nighttime late. When the morning came, we got up. Father Flanagan was with us. Anyway, we boys gave our order of what we wanted for breakfast and put the order in. When we all were ready to go down, we went together to the restaurant. I most generally brought up the back end because I liked to window shop and trail along behind.

"So when I came into this restaurant, the fellow said he wanted the little colored boy to eat in the kitchen. Father asked him why. He said, 'Well we don't serve any colored people in this town.' That town only had about three or four colored in it at that time. They were the janitors of the banks or the shoeshine fellows or something like that. Father said, 'Okay.' And we all went to the kitchen.

"Then the man said, 'I don't mean all of you – just the little colored boy.' Father Flanagan turned around and said, 'Well, if the boy can't eat out [t]here, and we can't eat in here, then

we don't eat here at all.' He turned around and he left the food
– they had a table all set and everything, the food was all
cooked and waiting for us – and he walked out.

"That same night, when we did our show, that restaurant
owner came in and donated $500 to the cause."

A few years before his death, Father Flanagan received a
letter from a Michigan priest praising him for his "inter-racial
good will" in the founding and running of his home. Father
Flanagan replied:

"I know when the idea of a boys' home grew in my mind,
I never thought of anything remarkable about taking in all of
the races and all the creeds. To me, they are all God's children.
They are my brothers. They are children of God. I must protect
them to the best of my ability and these Negro boys have been
just as fine and decent as the boys of my race and I have never
suffered by too much criticism from any of my friends because
of this inter-racial good will, which I must have as a Christian
and Catholic. ...

"... I do not consider myself doing anything remarkable. I
am only trying to do the Will of God.

"Who am I that I should think that Christ, when he died
on Calvary, died only for the Catholics living on millionaire
row and white Catholics at that. My understanding of Catholic
doctrine is that Christ died for the Negroes, for the Mexicans,
for the Germans and for the Japanese, and for all of these other
nationalities, and why should I, therefore, set up a church and
become a dictator as a Pastor in that church, and say that my
church is exclusively for the white race and that the Negro
must not worship here. That would smack of the attitude of

the Innkeepers when Mary and Joseph entered into the little town of Bethlehem and were greeted with the answer, 'There is no room.'

"I think one of the most remarkable and outstanding results of the gift of Faith in the Negro is the fact that he has persevered in spite of the opposition he has received. He must be very close to Christ and he knows something of what the Cross that Christ carried, signifies. He carries it, he must know."

Interview with Oscar Flakes, December, 1988, Girls and Boys Town Hall of History archives.
Letter to Rev. J.E. Coogan, S.J., Detroit, Michigan, September 22, 1945, Girls and Boys Town Hall of History archives.

CHAPTER FIVE

'No Such Thing as a Bad Boy'

Many times during his years of operating his Home for Boys, Father Flanagan spoke out passionately in defense of young boys who had committed violent crimes. He vehemently opposed society's common reaction of locking them up in prison or placing them on death row. In the following excerpt from a 1930s radio program, Flanagan explained why he saw no sense in such harsh punishment of young offenders.

✳✳

I READ IN THE PAPER the other day the story of a fifteen-year-old boy under arrest for murder – killing a man during a holdup. The boy is being charged with first-degree murder. The controversy over the charge is waxing warm.

Some people insist that the boy should not be tried as a hardened, adult criminal. Others say the boy deserves the full penalty of the law.

Now, I am for a trial in this case – but I say – the right defendant is not being put on trial. The questions I want

Radio program scripts, Girls and Boys Town Hall of History archives.

answered are these: Who committed this crime? Was it the boy, who with a great deal of bravado aped some of his elders and went out to get some money the easy way? Was it the boy, nervous, ill-guided, who pulled the trigger in a nervous reaction?

Or, shouldn't we ask ourselves: Is it the boy's parents who were responsible? Was it his teachers? Was it the cop on the beat in the boy's own neighborhood? Was it his companions? Or, was it society?

That boy did not come into the world predisposed to crime, not by any manner of means. When that boy was a babe, he was as much a potential good citizen, a leader, as any babe who ever grew up to be a good citizen and leader.

When, then, did he go wrong – where did the bad influence turn him to crime and to murder and to the prospect of facing the chair or life imprisonment at an age when most kids are still going to school or playing games? If we can answer that question perhaps we can decide who should be on trial.

Did the boy's parents give him that out of life which he should have – not merely some sort of existence, a little food, a few rags, a place to throw himself to sleep? Did they do anything about building up his ideals, about instilling self-respect, love or decency, friendship for his fellow man, belief in God?

And his teachers, did they pause in their duties to do more than set up an arithmetic assignment for him to do and to punish him and label him as incorrigible when he committed some minor wrong? Did they try to understand him and have time for sympathetic, human relationship?

Did the policeman walking his beat in the poor neighborhood in which little Johnny lived, make a friend of Johnny, teach him to respect the law, let him know that the police were his friends, or did he run the little boy off the streets and predict a bad end for him?

Was there proper, organized recreation provided for his neighborhood? Or did the street gangs run his end of town?

And what part did society play in making the boy feel he was part of a "good, healthy" society, that he and his fellows had a place in making a better world, that he was growing into a self-respecting, society-respecting man?

We must answer these questions before we put this youngster on trial – and I think I have the answers: The parents just didn't care much how the boy grew up; the teachers were too swamped with work and hundreds of other children to even think of helping this one boy; the cop on the beat thought his job was to keep the kids in fear of him; society went its willful, unregarding way – holding to the theory that the threat of punishment should keep people good.

Now, who should be on trial? Certainly not this misguided youngster who can't differentiate between right and wrong.

⛥⛥

In another radio speech, given on June 13, 1926, Father Flanagan explained how his home could offer such boys an alternative to soul-deadening years in reform school or prison.

FATHER FLANAGAN'S BOYS' HOME was started for the purpose of assisting poor boys between the ages of ten and fifteen years of age who were found to be suffering from neglect and who had no parents to care for them or bad parents who were not caring for them. You cannot expect to develop good citizenship from neglected boys if you allow them to remain neglected, but you can breed from neglected boys types of criminals who can become a danger and menace to society.

We all realize what a detriment the criminal is to society. He won't work and is, therefore, not a producer and hence, adds nothing to the well-being and prosperity of society. He must eat and usually supplies himself with the necessaries and luxuries of life by stealing, robbing, murdering all who come in his path who would prevent him, thus causing endless amount of destruction to property, and, in the wake of that path, broken-hearted and helpless widows and orphans. His cost to society cannot be estimated in dollars and cents for, with them in the balance must be weighed, too, the tears and sufferings, the sad heart over-powered with grief wherever his hand of death has dealt its blow.

Sending neglected boys to reform schools to furnish them a home is not a good thing because these poor boys need a home and training that will develop them into useful citizens, and they do not need to have the stamp of the reform school placed on them as a constant reminder of their once neglected condition.

Such boys must be dealt with the greatest kindness and prudence and with an understanding of their condition which will eliminate theorizing. There is no time for discussing what is wrong with this boy or that, especially after he has suffered for years perhaps. Feed the poor child good wholesome food and plenty of it; talk to him about anything and everything except himself, and you will soon arouse an interest in that poor lad which will be the awakening of his dormant soul.

If a home such as Father Flanagan's Boys' Home can save even one neglected boy who had been going headlong towards a life of crime, it would be justifiable for all the expense in maintaining it and the sacrifice made on the part of those engaged in the work. We do not claim that this home is going to be the panacea for all crime, but we do feel that with the years and with the cooperation of the good citizenship of the country, this home will do its part towards helping to stem the tide of crime and vice and the citizenship of tomorrow will be enriched because of it.

⊁⊁

On what principles of child rearing and youth work did Father Flanagan base his care of neglected children? He outlined his approach in a September 13, 1929, speech in St. Paul to the Minnesota State Conference of Social Workers.

... ALTHOUGH WE CAN NEVER rid society entirely of the delinquent boy or girl, we can do wonderful work with the individual; we can restore moral and mental health to thousands and thousands of boys and girls, and thus reopen for them the avenues of hope and encouragement that will eventually lead them into lives of utility and righteousness.

How can we do this? Let me explain one method through the medium of a concrete case: my Home for Boys. As I have said before, we have been exceptionally successful, and yet we have no special remedy or cure. We have, however, certain ideals that we invariably follow. I shall try to briefly explain them to you.

Fundamental to a boy's proper development we consider his physical needs and health. No boy comes into the Home without a thorough physical examination. No efforts are spared to correct any defects that may be found. Bad tonsils and adenoids are removed; poor teeth are put into condition; eyes are tested and treated, and any other bodily ailments are properly and immediately taken care of. We believe that the health of the boy is fundamental to his proper mental and moral development. In accordance with this health policy, the food supply is carefully watched to assure that each boy gets a sufficient amount of substantial food. Supervised exercise is also given to them daily. This not only is a factor leading towards health, but is also an excellent means of occupying the time of the boy. I am a firm believer in the old saying that "Idleness is the cradle of crime," and so I make it a point that my boys are kept occupied at all times.

… [O]ur solicitude for his physical needs does not, however, extend merely to those of the present. We likewise look forward to his needs of the future. All social workers recognize the fact that regardless of the excellent physical, mental, and moral training we give a boy, that unless we teach him a means of making a livelihood when he gets out in the world, we cannot expect him to live up to his principles of right and honesty. A hungry stomach has no master, and consequently we cannot expect the boy to live as a respectable citizen unless we teach him the means of satisfying the natural needs of his body. With this thought in mind we give each boy not only a grade school education, and a commercial course, but likewise insist that he is taught a remunerative trade. At the Home, therefore, we provide for him the facilities to learn either carpenter work, farming, shoemaking, engineering, printing, or music. I am convinced this trade work is a most important factor in bringing about the great success of so many boys in later life.

... [I]n addition to the care of the physical needs of the boy, we are very solicitous about his mental and spiritual life. In conformity with this ideal we give him not only an education ..., but also, at all times both in the classroom and out of it we persist in instilling in his mind and heart a knowledge of right and wrong, and an understanding of the principles of honesty, truth and morality, motivated by a realization of the existence of a True God to whom he owes both his obedience and homage. Not only do we teach him what is right and wrong, but also show him why it is so. When we tell a boy he must not steal, we also show why he must not do so; when we tell him lying is wrong, we add a reason for it; when we tell him that honesty is a necessary virtue, we tell him also, why it is.

This brings us to a very important phase, namely that of motives. We are all actuated by motives which may be classified as material and spiritual. The former constitute negative and positive motives. Among these negative motives we have fear of the law, and punishment, poverty, hunger, lack of comfort, terms in reform schools and penitentiaries. These negative motives may be very vividly and effectively presented, but should not be stressed too much to effect reform or reconstruction. Positive motives are far more effective, such as love of Country, wealth, success, family pride, respect of friends and associates. These afford to the mind some definite reward to look forward to. It is surprising how much one can do with the young lad by presenting to him in a frank and open-bodied manner the different material motives for right living. As a rule his heart is right, his mind impressionable, and he will respond especially if he considers you his sincere friend.

CHAPTER SIX

 # THE TOUGHEST KID HE EVER KNEW

"There is no such thing as a bad boy." Even though Father Flanagan believed this with his whole heart, some boys were harder to reach than others. He shared the story of one of the toughest kids he ever cared for with Fulton and Will Oursler who recounted it in their biography of Father Flanagan.

✷✷

ONE WINTER NIGHT A LONG-DISTANCE phone call came to Boys Town.

"Father Flanagan? This is Sheriff Hosey – from Virginia. Got any room for another boy – immediately?"

"Where is he now?"

"In jail. He's a desperate character – robbed a bank, held up three stores with a revolver ----"

"How old is he?"

"Eight and a half!"

The gaunt, blue-eyed priest stiffened at the telephone.

From *Father Flanagan of Boys Town*, by Fulton Oursler and Will Oursler, copyright © 1949, by Fulton Oursler and Will Oursler. Used by permission of Doubleday, a division of Random House, Inc.

"He's what?"

"Don't let his age fool you. He's all I said he was and more. Will you take him off our hands?"

"If I can't manage an eight-and-one-half-year-old child by this time, I ought to quit," he said unguardedly. "Bring him out!"

Three days later, near the end of a cheerless afternoon, Sheriff Hosey and his red-faced wife set down their prisoner in Father Flanagan's office – an unnaturally pale boy with a bundle under his arm. He was no higher than the desk; frowzy hair of chocolate brown dangled over the pinched and freckled face – eyes shut beneath long dark lashes. From one side of his mouth a smoldering cigarette drooped at a theatrical angle.

"Don't mind the smoking," pleaded the sheriff. "We had to bribe him with cigarettes to behave himself."

Meanwhile the wife laid a long envelope on the desk.

"There's a complete report," she snapped. "And that's not the half of it. This good-for-nothing criminal is not worth helping – it's my personal opinion he ain't even human! Good-bye and good luck – you're going to need it!"

Looking upon this patched wraith of childhood, Flanagan thought that never had he seen such a mixture of the comical and the utterly squalid and tragic. But he could not foresee that during the next year all Boys Town would be plagued with the same godless mixture of belly laugh and heartbreak.

Waving the newcomer to a chair, the priest turned on the desk lamp and began to read. It seemed that people had forgotten the boy's last name; he was just Eddie. Born in a slum near the docks, he had lost father and mother in a flu epidemic before he was four. In water-front flats he was shunted from one family to another, living like a hungry and desperate little animal.

Hardship sharpened his cunning and his will. It was literally true that at the age of eight he became the boss of a gang of boys, some nearly twice his age. He dominated them, as older toughs of the neighborhood taught him to do; he browbeat them into petty crimes which he planned in logical detail.

But about six months before the law caught up with Eddie his rule was challenged by a new member of the gang:

"You never do anything yourself. You're no leader."

"I'll show you," replied Eddie. "I'll do something you wouldn't dare … I'm going to rob a bank."

The bank was housed in the basement of an old-fashioned building. When most of the clerks were away at lunch Eddie lowered himself through a window, entered unseen, and crossed to an unattended slot of the cashier cage. So small that he had to chin himself up, he thrust in one grimy paw, seized a packet of green bills, and hid them in his jacket. Then, with complete sang-froid, he walked into the street, to divide two hundred dollars among his comrades. But the exploit was a flop; the bank concealed the theft, and there were no headlines.

"You're only cracking your jaw," the gang jeered. "You found that dough somewhere."

For several days Eddie vanished from his favorite street corner. Some vicious oldster had sold him a Colt revolver and stuffed his pockets with bullets; for two days Eddie stayed in the fields beyond town, practicing marksmanship.

This time the local front pages were full of him. Slouching into a restaurant at an empty hour, he aimed his gun at the terrified counterman while his other palm received a day's take from the cash register. Next he dragged a cabbage of bills from the pants pocket of a shivering tailor. His third call was on an old lady who kept a candy store.

"Put down that thing," this grandmother cried, "before you hurt yourself!"

She smacked the gun out of his hand and grabbed him by the hair. Like an insensate little demon, he began to struggle; he might have killed her, but her screams brought policemen. Now Eddie had wound up in Boys Town.

Putting aside the manuscript, Father Flanagan looked musingly at the villain of the piece. From this night on the past must be a closed book; the idea was to forget it and start over again.

But certain things were already clear. This was not a villain but a victim. Born under another roof, Eddie could have been another kind of boy, knowing the sweetness of home, birthday candles, Christmas parcels, mother's tender vigilance – yes, and the strong, wise counsel of a father's pride.

Something else showed in the report: Eddie had resourcefulness and a realistic brain; one must respect his intelligence and appeal to it.

"No matter what he says or does," Father Flanagan resolved, "I'll never give up until I've won him over."

In the dimmish light Eddie stood unmoving, head lowered, looking at the floor; it was hard to see much of that pale wrinkled face. But as the man watched, the child produced a small piece of white paper and a sack of Bull Durham. One-hand-cowboy fashion, he deliberately rolled his own cigarette and, having lighted it, thumbnail to match, he blew a plume of smoke billowing across the desk.

Then long eyelashes lifted for a flash, to see how the priest was taking the exhibition; Father Flanagan's first sight of those bright brown eyes.

"Eddie," began the leader of Boys Town, "you are welcome here. The whole place is run by the fellows, you know. Boy mayor. Boy city council. Boy chief of police."

"Where's the jail?" grunted Eddie in basso profundo.

"We haven't a jail. You are going to take a bath and then get supper. Tomorrow you start in school. You and I can become real friends – it's strictly up to you. I love you and someday I hope I can take you to my heart. I know you're a good boy!"

The reply came in a single shocking syllable.

About eleven o'clock next morning Father Flanagan, smiling ruefully, was looking over the inventory of Eddie's bundle – a few odds and ends of shirts, unmatching socks, a fresh pair of drawers, and a white rabbit's foot – when the door to the office opened and the new pupil swaggered in. His hair had been cut and neatly combed and he was clean. With an air of great unconcern he tossed on the desk a note from one of the teachers:

Dear Father Flanagan:

We have heard you say a thousand times that there is no such thing as a bad boy. Would you mind telling me what you call this one?

Back in that classroom the atmosphere was about as cheerful as Mother's Day in the death house. The teacher described how Eddie had sat quietly in his seat for about an hour;

suddenly he began parading back and forth in the aisle, swearing like a longshoreman and throwing movable objects on the floor, finally pitching an ink-well, which landed accurately on a plaster bust of Cicero.

Replacing Eddie in his seat, Father Flanagan apologized:

"It was my fault … I never told him he mustn't throw ink-wells. The laws of Boys Town will, of course, be enforced with him, as with all the rest of us. But he has to learn them first. We must never forget that Eddie is a good boy."

"Like hell I am!" screamed Eddie.

The child seemed made of stone. He made no friends among boys or teachers, least of all with Father Flanagan, for whom he reserved his supreme insult, picked up God knows where – "a damned praying Christian." Spare time he spent roaming about stealthily, looking for a chance to run away. Sullenly he stood aloof in gymnasium and on baseball and football fields: "Kid stuff!" Neither choir nor band could stir him; the farm bored him.

Given the slightest chance at freedom, he showed himself proudly unregenerate – upsetting a jigsaw puzzle laboriously put together, tearing a book apart with his bare hands, and, in the midst of class prayers, mewing like a cat.

And in all that first six months not once a laugh, nor a tear. Soon the one question in Boys Town was whether Father Flanagan had met his match at last.

"Does the little guy learn anything?" he asked the sisters.

"Somehow he is getting his ABCs," they reported. "In fact,

he's learning more than he lets on. But he's just eaten up with hate!"

One night an older boy reported that Eddie was groaning in his sleep. Walking into the dormitory, Father Flanagan stood beside the bed, touched the flushed face and felt the warm sweat of fever,

"Just a sick little boy," he thought penitently. "It is shameful and foolish of me to lose hope. How can a little boy be bad when he is so soon from God?"

Perhaps the Lord had been trying him out with Eddie, to see how deep was his faith.

"Well, I'm going to take all He wants to send – with the help of God, of course!" he added hastily.

There must be something in Eddie that could be worked out. By the ruddy name of Flanagan he would find it!

Through dark and gusty grounds the priest walked that October night, his grieving face set against the wind. It came to him then how real fathers must feel toward little sons. Sometimes they love so much that they spoil them. Eddie had been spoiled, all right, but not that way.

"I'll have to throw away the book of rules," grumbled Flanagan. "I'm going to try spoiling the little devil with love!"

As he reached this peak of noble intention a blast blew off his hat and for a quarter of an hour he was on his knees, prowling among the bushes.

In the infirmary Eddie snarled at the doctors, but when they accused him of being afraid he swallowed the medicine without a grimace; he walked into the darkness of the X-ray chamber with the air of a condemned man unbroken as he marched to the chair.

Well again, he became more silent than ever. An apathy settled upon him just when the leader of the village was giving him more attention than he had ever given anyone else. Boys and teachers began to watch the new strategy as if it were a contest; a sporting proposition, and the home team was Father Flanagan.

Upon these weeks and months he looked back with a reminiscent shudder, especially at the scores of B-picture programs they sat through, all double features. It is still a medical wonder that Eddie did not get ulcers from hot dogs and hamburgers, nut and chocolate bars, peanut brittle, ice cream, Coca-Cola, Pepsi-Cola, and tonics of thirty rainbow colors. Inside his puny body there lay some cavernous area capable of infinite absorption.

Yet never once did Eddie say that anything was fun or sweet or refreshing; never a remark came unprompted; all answers briefly severe. In summer dawns, smelling of pines and wild clover, he would trudge stolidly down to the lake, but no grunt of excitement came when he landed a trout. After each private excursion he would leave Father Flanagan with the same overbearing smile.

Only once toward the end of that unhappy experiment did man and boy come closer together. That was at a street crossing in Omaha when Eddie was looking in the wrong direction and a truck tore around a corner; Father Flanagan yanked him out of harm's way. For one instant a light of gratitude flickered in the startled brown eyes, then the lashes fell again; he said nothing.

Stalemate! Even to the man of faith it began to seem that here was an inherent vileness beyond his reach. Hope had fallen to the lowest possible point when one soft spring morning Eddie boldly appeared in the office, announcing that he wanted to have it out with Father Flanagan. This time the brown eyes were glowing with indignation.

"You've been trying to get around me," he began, "but now I'm wise to you. If you was on the level, I might have been a sucker at that. I almost fell for your line. But last night I got to thinking it over, and I sees the joker in the whole thing."

There was something terribly earnest and manful in Eddie now; this was not insolence but despair. With a stab of hope the priest noticed for the first time a quiver on the twisted lips.

"Father Flanagan, you're a phony!"

"You better prove that, Eddie – or shut up!"

"Okay! I just kicked a Sister in the shins. Well? Now what do you say?"

"I still say you are a good boy."

"What did I tell you? You keep on saying that lie, and you know it's a lie, it can't be true – doesn't that prove you're a phony?"

Dear Father in heaven, this is honest logic! How can I answer it? How defend my faith in him – and in You? Because it's now or never with Eddie – God give me the grace to say the right thing.

Father Flanagan cleared his throat.

"Eddie, you're smart enough to know when a thing is really proved. What is a good boy? A good boy is an obedient boy. Right?"

"Yeah."

"Does what his teachers tell him to do?"

"You bet!"

"Well, that's all you've ever done, Eddie. The only trouble with you is that you had the wrong teachers – wharf toughs and corner bums – but you have certainly obeyed them; you've done every last wrong and rotten thing they taught you to do. If you could only obey the good teachers here in the same way, you'd be just fine!"

Those simple words of unarguable truth were like an exorcism, driving out devils from the room and cleansing the air. At first the tiny human enigma looked dumbfounded. Then came a glisten of sheer downright relief in the brown eyes, and he began to creep around the side of the sunlit desk. And with the very same relief Father Flanagan's soul was crying; he held out his arms and the child climbed into them and laid a tearful face against his heart.

That was a long time ago. For ten years Eddie remained in Boys Town, until, well near the top of his class, he left to join the United States Marines. On blood-smeared beaches he won three promotions.

"His chest," boasted Father Flanagan, "is covered with medals. Nothing strange about that, though; no wonder he has courage. But God be praised for something else; he has the love of the men in his outfit – brother to the whole bunch he is – an upstanding Christian character. And still the toughest kid I ever knew!"

CHAPTER SEVEN

'He Loved Me as a Boy'

One of the best-remembered films of 1938 was MGM's now-classic "Boys Town." Studded with stars like Spencer Tracy portraying Father Flanagan and Mickey Rooney playing the tough, streetwise kid Whitey Marsh, the film won two Academy Awards (including one for Tracy's performance) and drew box office lines across the country. Newspapers reported people standing in line for hours to buy movie tickets as well as people emerging from the theaters sobbing, only to get back in line to see the second show.

The cast and crew spent ten sweltering summer days on the Boys Town campus for location shooting. Tracy was so impressed with Flanagan and the boys' home that he later gave Flanagan his Oscar with this added inscription: "To Father Edward Joseph Flanagan whose great human qualities, kindly simplicity and inspiring courage were strong enough to shine through my humble efforts. Spencer Tracy."

Another member of the cast was child star Bobs Watson who portrayed PeeWee, the pint-sized boy who hero-worships the brash-talking Whitey. Although only seven years old at the time,

Watson found his real-life hero in Father Flanagan. Leaving acting behind as an adult, Watson became a United Methodist minister and credited Father Flanagan as the inspiration behind his life-changing decision.

In 1990, the Rev. Bobs Watson revisited the Boys Town campus to deliver the sermon at the dedication of the newly built Chambers Protestant Chapel. In his remarks, he remembered Father Flanagan:

✄

"I CAME UP TO BOYS TOWN as a seven-year-old boy, and I saw this beautiful man, tall – I had to look way up to him. And the day that I first saw him he was wearing one of those straw hats because it was so bloomin' hot here. He looked down at me, and I was introduced to him. Later I came to find out as a boy finds things out that this is the man who said, 'There is no such thing as a bad boy.' Now that's hope. …

"Father Flanagan was the kind of a man [who] gave love unbelievably. I remember standing not too far from here, just in front of where the administration building was at one time. I remember that it was hot, and I remember that he was standing out there talking with some men who had come here from Hollywood and from Wall Street to see how the film was progressing. And I remember … watching one of his little children come up to him and pull on his pant leg. And he stopped and he turned … his back on [the men] to attend to the needs of his children.

"Seventeen thousand children have gone through here because of one man. Because of one man who built his life upon a rock, a rock that would never diminish and a rock that was based upon love. … What I remember of Father Flanagan was, he loved me, not as an actor – he loved me as a boy. He loved me and I loved him back. And I thought, how can this be? He's Catholic. …

"But Father Flanagan loved a Protestant boy, and that Protestant boy never forgot what he gave to him. … I can no longer look at children as Bobs Watson, the little actor, would have looked at people if he grew up. … Now I look at children in the light that I saw Father Flanagan look at people. … Children are people with hopes and dreams, and sometimes their lives are made of mud and slush and the memories are bad …

"But here they find love, and it was possible because of a man who had the courage to stand up and love children, no matter what. And upon the rock of Jesus Christ, he built this place. He built it with love and now all of us have the opportunity to continue the giving of that love. You see … we are all children of God, and Father Flanagan knew that. He changed my whole outlook on life … and he made me the Protestant that God intended me to be. He gave me the love to love him back without reservation."

[In one of the movie's climactic scenes, Whitey decides to leave Boys Town. A crying PeeWee follows, begging Whitey to take him along, and runs into the street where he is hit by a car.]

"Little PeeWee has endeared himself to the world, not because of me, … but because of that unique little gift that was given to a seven-year-old child, to reach out with love to Whitey Marsh. … Whitey Marsh is a very tough little guy who comes to Boys Town, doesn't believe in God or people. …

Father Flanagan tried to give him all that he could of the love of God ... [but] Whitey was leaving ... to have a life that would probably be destroyed. But Father Flanagan had already instilled that love into someone else, a little innocent child, [PeeWee, who] could not see the pain and the misery and the hurt and all of the anger that was in Whitey. And he ran after him as a pal, because he loved him.

"Do you know what happened Thursday, before I left to come here? I sat down and I watched *Boys Town* again. And suddenly something struck me in one of those lines that I said fifty-two years ago ... that the reason why PeeWee and Whitey had such a union ... is because PeeWee, the character, epitomized the simplistic love of God for Whitey when he said, 'But, Whitey, I want to go with you.' Whitey was leaving without ... the love of God, and that is what little PeeWee exemplified. ...

"And so I give you my simple message from my heart, not from an actor, but from a PeeWee. ... I leave you with what I know God wants everyone to feel when they have been to this place and leave. ... I want to go with you. May the peace, may the love of God be upon all of us."

Sermon by Rev. Bobs Watson, June 24, 1990, Chambers Protestant Chapel, Boys Town, Nebraska, Girls and Boys Town Hall of History archives.

CHAPTER EIGHT

THE NEED FOR PRAYER

"Every boy must pray, how he prays is up to him," Father Flanagan believed. Boys of all faiths were admitted to Boys Town, and Father Flanagan always respected the religious tradition from which each boy came. What he did insist upon, however, was that every boy regularly pray and practice his individual faith. Religion, he believed, was the cornerstone of a life of good character. In the following essay, he explains why, how, and when children should pray.

✤✤

I HAVE BEEN SPEAKING TO YOU through this page for the last few months about the things that you must do in life, and about the things that you must avoid doing, if you wished to grow up into honest and respectable men, dear to your fellowmen and dear to your God. I have tried in as simple a way as possible to explain to you some of the Ten Commandments,

---

"Little Talks to Children," by Edward J. Flanagan, *Father Flanagan's Boys' Home Journal,* Copyright © 1930, Father Flanagan's Boys' Home, September, 1930.

and I have exhorted you to obey these laws because of your love for that Great Father who has been so kind and generous with you.

Now, my dear children, you will find all the way through life, that great temptations will besiege you to violate these laws, and to be untrue to the love of God, your Creator and Master. I wish, therefore, today to speak to you about a very special way in which you may fortify yourself against these temptations. You must learn early in life that unaided you cannot withstand the many alluring temptations of life, and that you must in order to keep honest, and pure, and truthful seek the help of some Higher Force to aid and strengthen you. I want to speak to you at this time about the great and only certain method of obtaining help and strength, and that method is by prayer.

Prayer is the connecting link between God and man. It is the means by which we talk to God, tell Him of our needs, and ask Him for assistance. You well know, children, that we all depend upon God for everything. Of ourselves we are helpless, and we have to look to God for that assistance which we need. Unless we ask Him for the strength and grace to be good and to persevere in that goodness, we need not expect God to give us that help. As little children you all loved to pray to God. You loved to be good, and holy, and you dreaded doing anything that would offend that Great Goodness. You were happy, and your happiness seemed to reflect on all who knew you. Do you remember those wonderful years when you were little tots praying at your mother's knee? Do you remember how devout you were, and how happy? At that time you depended on God for everything; you had perfect trust and faith in Him.

But as the years passed on, you remarked a change come over you. As you grew stronger in body and wiser in mind, you commenced to look upon life differently, and began, too, to take some credit to yourselves for your growth in mind and body. Your companions, too, flattered you, and I fear it helped to turn your mind a little bit, and with the change you became somewhat cold and indifferent to God in return for all His goodness to you. As a result you also changed in your attitude toward your parents. You are not as considerate of them now as formerly. When you thus begin to drift away from the most sacred and helpful of influences, and start to trust yourselves on your own resources of helplessness, is the time my dear boys and girls, when more than at any other you need to increase your devotion to God, and more earnestly to petition Him for the grace and strength to grow up into good spiritual men and women.

Always remember your own helplessness; for this thought will humble you in God's sight, and dispose you better to plead with Divine Justice for the help you stand most in need. Remember, too, your paths are beset with many snares and traps to drag you down to a life of sin and vice, and to a life of failure. Oh! So many young folks have listened and followed the call of their enemies, and have left the path of God, to become the enemies of God and in turn to tempt others away from Him. From this class we have our criminals, bad and vicious people who are a scourge to society and who are infesting it with their poison.

What you need, dear boys and girls, is more prayer. Prayer, that will strengthen you to resist temptations, and keep you from falling away from the helpful, holy, and sacred influences which alone will save and preserve you. If you form the habit of prayer, you will find that it is a refreshing balm to your troubled hearts and minds, and a great consolation and help in time of trouble and temptation.

Now, for what things should you pray? First of all, your spiritual welfare – it is your first and most important consideration. Your immortal souls came from God, belong to Him, and they must return to Him. Sin, that great monster in the eyes of God, is the only thing that separates your souls from God. For this, therefore, should you pray first, last, and all the time, that God give you strength and grace to remain always in His friendship, and hold a place in His Divine Heart. Then you may pray for your parents, friends, and benefactors that God will save and preserve them, and likewise give them strength and grace to resist temptation to sin and vice. You may pray for temporal favors, such as success in life, your individual enterprises in life, provided such requests are pleasing to Almighty God. You know, sometimes, people pray to God for some favors that they consider should be granted, but remember God is under no obligation to any of His creatures, and is not bound by anyone. Then, too, what may seem good to you, may not seem good to the All-seeing mind of God, and so, if you pray for something, and your prayers are not answered, you should not be discouraged, for God knows best. Again God may not grant your requests immediately, but keep you in suspense in order to test your faith in Him. In any case you should keep on praying and never give up in despair.

And now we may ask, how should you pray? When you pray, you speak to God or to God's special friends who will intercede to Him for you. Now children, think of the privilege that is yours to converse with God. Isn't it a really wonderful privilege? You and I would consider it a great honor to speak with some great personage, such as the President of the United States, and our behavior in his presence would be such as to please him. Since it is our privilege in prayer to speak to the King of Kings and Lord of Hosts, who holds in the very hollow of His Hands this great country of ours, and its Presidents as well, we should be most mindful of praying with every attention and devotion, and thus by our deep humility give honor and glory to God on whom we entirely depend and from whom we expect so many favors and blessings.

When should you pray? Always. This does not mean that you should do nothing else but remain in prayer and meditation all day and neglect your other duties. No – but as you depend on God for everything, you should always be so disposed that the habit of prayer should be so acquired that everything you do during the day should ascend to Heaven as a sweet incense to honor God, and to request Him for His help. In particular, however, should you spend some time each morning and night in prayer, and also during times of temptation, trials and sorrows, at which times you especially need Divine Help.

Now, my dear children, I want all of you to pray more, and pray with greater attention and devotion. You know, God loves you very much, so much that He sent down His only Divine Son from Heaven to live on earth, to suffer and die for you, so you would be saved. The all-loving Heart of God is overflowing with love and sympathy for His poor suffering children here on earth, and is ever ready to listen to your requests and pleadings for aid to keep within the bounds of His Grace and Friendship. Do not, therefore, neglect Him. Do not disappoint Him, and your success in this life as well as your eternal salvation will be assured. This is the true and only remedy for our individual and social ills.

CHAPTER NINE

 # THE CAUSES OF JUVENILE DELINQUENCY

In the 1930s and '40s, Father Flanagan became one of the most-respected voices in America on juvenile delinquency, its causes, and how to prevent it. He gave dozens of speeches – to local clubs, social agencies, charitable organizations, and even the U.S. Senate. He was also called in by state and local governments to look at and suggest reforms at other juvenile facilities, such as the Whittier State School in California and the Boys Vocational School in Lansing, Michigan.

Following is a speech he gave in 1939 to probation and parole officers. In it he touches on themes that were central to his beliefs: the family as the primary unit of society, the importance of religion in daily life and in the rehabilitation of troubled children, the role of school and community in the socialization and support of children, and the court's responsibility to encourage rehabilitation rather than punishment in most cases of juvenile delinquency.

... THE ALARMING PROPORTIONS of our annual crime tell the spectacle of reformatories and prisons crowded to the bursting point, and the misery and heartbreak which attend these conditions, invite the earnest consideration of every thinking American. Sixteen billions of dollars of our national wealth goes annually to fill the coffers of crime. Reformatories take in large numbers of our youth, support them at the expense of the taxpayer, and turn them loose later as more efficient predatory animals. Prisons incarcerate the casual offender with the recidivist. The stupendous funds, which go into the maintenance of this system, are as a torrent beside the thin trickle of public money which goes into prevention. The situation is nothing less than obnoxious.

The physician treating a series of grave disorders does not use isolation exclusively. The doctor who would quarantine for every disease would be nothing short of a fool. The wise physician gathers his data, correlates his technical knowledge, applies all of his skill, and looks toward an eventual cure. In the rare, and constantly growing rarer, cases where a cure is not to be expected, he segregates his patient from society. I submit that the same procedure can be followed in dealing with crime, and I insist that it must be followed if we are to secure anything approaching the cure of this tremendous evil. Our civilization is a social body, and that body is seriously ill.

The causes of juvenile delinquency and adult crime are not shrouded in mystery. We know them, and we know them for what they are. We know what we may expect of them, and we are as well acquainted with the means of cure. Yet progress lags

---

Speech by Edward J. Flanagan to Central States Probation and Parole Conference, St. Louis, Missouri, April 30, 1939, from Girls and Boys Town Hall of History archives.

behind proved theory in a most disturbing fashion. Knowledge is power, and yet in the field of crime and delinquency prevention it is a source very largely untapped. I have been interested in the practical application of probation since the hour of my ordination. I have put it to the test in over twenty years of practice, and I know its merits. I have no doubt that if the months or years before parole were more sanely and more efficiently handled, it would be as effective also. But with twenty-two years of wrestling with the problem in its individual aspects behind me, I cannot help but think that we would be wisely employed to deal with the situation before probation and parole become necessary, effective as those weapons are.

Publicly, we are now in the position of a physician who blinds his eyes to all disorders until they become malignant and require heroic treatment. We might better concentrate our attention on the first manifestations of the disease, and better still, we might bend our efforts toward keeping the social body healthy, and preventing occurrence of the malady.

Crime begins in the cradle. I have no less an authority than the chief of the Federal Bureau of Investigation for that statement, and I know from my own experience that it is true. What is more and worse, I know that only too many parents are not concerned with that vital truth. And yet, seeing the wreckage which negligent homes are casting upon the social sea, I cannot help but wonder why parental information is not more widely diffused, and why we do not insist that young people contemplating marriage have some knowledge, at least, of the responsibilities entailed in the marital venture. Men do not presume to enter upon the most inconsequential of tasks without some technical knowledge, and yet young men and young women embark upon society's most vital career in the blindest and blandest of ignorance.

The static character of maturity does not swerve from a well-ordered life to an anti-social career. The prelude to all adult crime is juvenile delinquency, and the factors which make for juvenile delinquency are common to the lives of all children. There is nothing in the abnormal considered socially or otherwise, which does not exist in the normal, either latently or mildly expressed. There is no fundamental difference between the latest reformatory commitment, and the son of the most upright and dignified citizen within the sound of my voice. The possibilities and potentialities for social living in both are on an absolute par. The difference is simply this: the upright citizen's son has been trained in social living, by his father, mother, church, school, and environment – the reformatory boy has been incorrectly trained, or he has been utterly neglected. The one has gained his knowledge of life and living in a well-ordered home, from kind and sympathetic and socially conscious parents. His problems have been met and dealt with as they arose, rationalized and thus dissipated. The reformatory boy gained his knowledge on the streets and in the alleys, from sources often vicious. His philosophy was formulated in the tenement, the poolroom, at cheaply sensational movies, and cribbed from the lascivious and erotic literature with which our newsstands reek.

Since crime begins in the cradle, any attempt to halt its onward march will have to begin there. Parents, and all of us, need to awaken to the fact that children need much more than food, and clothes, and shelter. Merely serving the physical needs of the child will go far toward training it for the social side of life, but it will fall far short of being far enough. Children have mental lives to lead as well as a physical existence to be sustained. They begin to form habits from the moment of their births – habits *mentally* dictated – and unless proper training is begun at once, the results can hardly be fortunate. Too often modern parents regard the very small child with something of the affection in which they would hold a puppy. They provoke demonstrations of affection and exhibitions of alleged ability, never stopping to consider that such exhibitionism may be harmful. They tolerate any line of conduct as long as it does not seriously interfere with their own convenience. The family is a definite social unit – it is a miniature world, and the habits gained in its circle are carried over into the larger world outside. Habit formation in the very tender years is of the utmost importance. Anti-social tendencies exhibit themselves at a very early age. They are nurtured by neglect, and fostered by pampering. And yet they can be trained and directed into mentally healthful and socially acceptable channels, quite as readily as they can be neglected.

The right of every child is to his home and all that a good home means. The responsibility of every parent, both in the natural and the supernatural order, is to give their children those practical lessons in every day social living which will develop them into the highest type of citizenry. This is not the time or place to delve into the problems of mental health, but I tell you that if the fundamental urges toward recognition, security, adventure, achievement and love are not met and properly interpreted in the home, the child will go beyond its confines to meet and interpret them for himself.

It is quite apparent that a great deal of delinquency – I should say a preponderantly major share of it – is the result of the abandonment of the home as the social unit, and the breakdown of family life. I need not necessarily speak in the character of a priest of God in stressing this fact. The family is the *natural* unit as well as the divinely appointed basis of human society. The moral law is an infallible guide to mental health and social living. The loose interpretation of it is the prelude to inevitable social chaos, of which delinquency is only one aspect. Divorce, desertion, hedonism, and family strife are as rotten in their results for society, as the moral leprosy, which causes them, is abhorrent to the moral mentally healthful mind.

I am aware that social service is a science. I know that it has stored up a fund of exact knowledge in the years of its development, and I know that it applies that knowledge to the solution of social problems. I know that all the services and agencies, which have grown out of that knowledge, have their places and serve their purposes in the social order. I hail the advances of social science, and I am sympathetic toward its every aim. But I tell you frankly and dispassionately, that any scheme of things, which leaves God and religion out of its considerations, is doomed to abysmal failure. God is the Author of life and it is He who must sustain it. He is the Support of the world and it is He who must order it. Unless and until He takes His rightful place in human affairs, we work in vain to right or to improve the order which He Himself established. Psychologists tell us and mental experts agree that religion can play a vital part in the rehabilitation of the maladjusted. I do not see this as strange; I cannot hail this as a major discovery. Religion is plainly and simply a rule of life – the great rule of life established by the Author of life itself. Success in any endeavor is not to be had by breaking or disregarding the rules.

The finest of homes cannot function to the best advantage without the influence of religion. Our social problems will not be solved until the home is re-established as the core and center of society. It is equally true that they will not be solved unless religion re-enters and revitalizes the family circle. Nations have fallen and whole cultures have vanished from the face of the earth through the neglect and the abandonment of these two all-important institutions. To paraphrase a verse of Scripture: "Unless God build the home, they labor in vain who build it." Unfortunately for our country, we do not have enough good homes. The cancer of divorce has eaten into the social body to an alarming degree, and the hectic pace of modern life goes far to neutralize the beneficent effects which even good homes confer upon society.

There is no single, central cause of delinquency and crime, and there is no panacea for their cure. True, the home is the basic social unit, and as such it contributes most heavily toward swelling the army of delinquents which is constantly passing through our courts. But the home acts and interacts with complementary agencies which have their own roles to play, and they, too, must function efficiently in delinquency prevention. The character training and education which makes for socially conscious adolescence and maturity must begin in the home, but it must be continued in the school and community.

The social contacts and experiences of school and community must be interpreted and evaluated in the home, by the father and mother. That is the ideal situation. Too frequently it does not obtain.

The school has a definite part to play in character education and citizenship training. Whatever the percentage of the child's time spent within the sphere of its influence – and it varies because of varying educational standards – a commensurate degree of responsibility must be borne for the good or bad citizenship and character which results. Surveys have shown that a large number of delinquents begin their anti-social careers with truancy. Unquestionably, in every instance, there are home and environmental factors at work. I am not unmindful of the fact that the truant runs to something, but I cannot escape the idea that he also runs *from* something. Friction results, of course, when immature judgments encounter social barriers, and school for the child is one of them. But this friction must be sublimated by some agency, and why should kindness and sympathetic interest not sublimate it at its source?

There is a wonderful opportunity for social service before every teacher. Where the pupil comes from a broken or negligent home, the school may be the only socializing influence the poor child encounters. Service to children must go beyond mere custodial care in the home, and it must exceed mere academic instruction in the school. Both home and school must prepare the child for more than life. Both must offer experiences and training in social living. Where are the criminals of ten years hence? They are in schoolrooms today. What shall we make of them? Liars and thieves, or socially conscious embryonic citizens. We shall have to bring teachers to the realization that they are more than mere pedants. They are social servants, and character is as much their business as it is that of parents.

The modern child has a vast amount of leisure at its disposal, when it is away from the influence of both home and school. We can accept its existence without going into the causes of it or the reasons for it. It exists because of a social and economic scheme of things, and the social body has obligations toward children because of it. I spoke a short while ago about fundamental urges, and gave it as my experience that where they are not socially fulfilled, children are prone to fulfill them in their own fashions. Much delinquency is the result of community neglect.

Under the present order of things we give little concern to possible centers of delinquency infection until the malady exhibits itself. Then we rush offenders to courts, and commit them to reformatories. Months later, perhaps, some volunteer organization, subsistent on charity, will come into the infected area, and establish itself to deal with a situation which has by this time become chronic. I have seen that happen more than once. We know that congested areas breed delinquency. We know that vice ridden sections contaminate. We know that children must have absorbing interests and room for healthful play. Why not anticipate? Why not move in advance upon such sections with our playgrounds, community centers, Boys' Clubs, Boy Scout troops and Girl Scout organizations? The community obligations exist, and the men and women volunteers can be secured and trained if the need for them is properly presented. Postponing activity until the infection breaks out is like locking the barn door after the horse is stolen. The *accent* on delinquency must be shifted to prevention, if it is to be prevented at all, and officialdom must pave the way for public emphasis upon that fact.

The solution of this problem cannot be left to prevention alone. There will always be those who will fail society, just as they have always existed. But even a large percentage of those unfortunates can be reclaimed and rehabilitated. I have spent over twenty years in proving it. We cannot do it with the social weapons we have at present. The ancient and creaking mills of justice need mightily to be overhauled. Legally, we have not come a great way from the child-hanging London court of a century ago. Even the juvenile court – and the mere fact that it exists is a hopeful sign and a humanitarian trend – is many times occupied exclusively with socially unimportant considerations. What does it consider? The *offense* – the *law* – the *penalty*. I am well aware that there are judges who use their offices for the good of society, and who look, in each case, toward an eventual cure. Their instances are so rare as to be considered newsworthy. Humanitarian procedure and the consideration of social welfare should be mandatory under the state constitutions. What does society want of the offender? Under the present legally established system it wants revenge, and under the established correctional process it gets it.

I quote from a legislative act in an eastern state. I shall not mention the source, for I have no wish to pillory this commonwealth. It differs in no essentials from its forty-seven sisters. The purpose of its Juvenile and Domestic Relations Court Act, as stated, is: "To secure for each child under its jurisdiction such care, guidance and control, preferably in his own home, as will conduce to the child's welfare and the best interests of the state; and when such child is removed from his own family, to secure for him custody, care and discipline as nearly as possible equivalent to that which should have been given by his parents." To quote further: "Children under the jurisdiction of the court are wards of the state, which may intervene to safeguard them from neglect or injury and to enforce the legal obligations due them, and from them."

This is noble, legally conceived theory. It is a step in the right direction. It is not as complete as it might be, and subject to wide interpretation. Still, it is sound reason and pregnant with possibilities. Unfortunately, it is unconstitutional. The judge who proceeds under those directions is violating the state constitution, which created his office. Social considerations move many judges to do just that. Constitutionally speaking, no judge is obliged to follow the dictates of that act. Legally, they may not free themselves from the atmosphere of criminal prosecution and methods which are largely punitive.

We need a constitutionally established definition of minority and minority offenses. We have a criminal code. But youngsters are not criminals. We need a code which will take their immature judgments into consideration, and interpret their social deviations without placing them in the same category as the confirmed, adult criminal. The status of the juvenile delinquent in law today, is a relic of the horse-and-buggy era, and wholly out of step with the progress we have made in the interpretation of juvenile behavior.

We need, as well, a constitutionally established definition of the powers and purposes of the juvenile court, and complete reform of judicial procedure as it affects the delinquent minor. The juvenile court, as I see it, should have a single aim, to insure the rehabilitation of as many offenders as is possible, and to dispose of the incorrigibles by segregating them from society. The judge of such a court will have to be as much of a clinician as he is a jurist and he will have to have the services of competent child experts at his command. Above and beyond all, the alleged correctional processes will have to be entirely revamped.

Today, hundreds of children are consigned to tax supported and state maintained schools of crime. Fully eighty percent of them can be rehabilitated. I refuse to believe that any more than twenty percent of our juvenile offenders are mentally so constituted as to find social living impossible. By far the greater number of our juvenile offenders can be reclaimed, and we shall take a great step forward when the reformatory is reformed. It is idle to suppose that mere incarceration can or will reform a character. Character springs from the will, and is the sum of habits often unconsciously formed. Repression, regimentation and harsh discipline can accomplish nothing, except deepen the anti-social sentiment and fix the criminal bent. Boys enter the reformatory in a fairly plastic state of mind. They leave, educated in crime and habituated to violence.

There is no excuse for this situation. Competent men can be had, proper training is available, but as long as the trend is toward punishment instead of cure, the fruit of the reformatory tree must inevitably be bitter. How ridiculously tragic it is, to use the public money to support a system which turns out human wolves to prey on the public.

The most hopeful sign of the times in the delinquency field is the use of probation and parole. They both spring from a Christian concept, and it is only the Christian philosophy, both in the life of the offender and in his social treatment, which can reclaim him for society. Until the day when the reforms I have indicated are brought into reality, we must work for the more widespread use of the only Christian procedure we now have available. Probation and parole fail only when politics takes a leprous hand in their administration. They must be taken from the political arena. The probation and parole officer, the reformatory staff member, the social case worker, are all too important to the life and well being of society to be the footballs of politicians. Their professional occupations must depend on what, not on who they know. They must be free to retain their professional integrity, and not be compelled to prostitute it for the base ends of political expediency. They must be public servants, not political pawns.

To speak of the proved merits of probation and parole is not my function. I have seen their benefits in countless cases which have been paroled to me, and I am sure that in each of your own lives, there are experiences and memories which fix the blessings of your professions in your minds and hearts forever.

In New York State, they tell me, one-fourth to one-eighth the amount necessary for incarceration, will provide the best and most efficient probation and parole supervision. The economic consideration is the least important one. Above all we must consider that probation and parole are the only *positive* measures we have available under the present antiquated legal tangle. No one wants to unleash predatory criminals and recidivists upon society. Least of all do you and I wish it. But we recognize the fact that human nature is prone to error, that we all make mistakes, and that it is much better for the state and society to teach boys and men to do right, than to attempt to forcibly restrain them from doing wrong.

I beg God's blessing upon this conference and upon all your work. It is truly a Christian pursuit – something almost analogous to the Good Shepherd – seeking the one – yes, the thousands who are lost – not leaving them to perish in the desert of social mismanagement and neglect. I call upon you and upon all Americans, for the sake of this country's future, to stand squarely behind every effort, from whatever source, which may improve the lot of our future citizens. I challenge the world to face the facts – your methods and mine – given an honest chance and sanely administered – always work. The old way always fails.

I look for a future – *not* free from crime – I know human nature too well for that. But I do look for one in which constantly enlarging circles of people will share our views – and the unfortunate youthful offender will claim his rightful share of attention and receive rightful consideration and beneficial treatment. We shall all be the better for the knowledge that God is the Father of us all, and that all of us – even the wayward – are His children.

CHAPTER TEN

 # To Cure, Not to Punish

Father Flanagan saw no sense in locking troubled children up in 'reformatories' where he believed they learned little more than how to commit additional crimes. In the speech reprinted below, he proposed a better way to deal with delinquents, one that focused on rehabilitation and, except in the most serious cases, avoided courts, jails, and reformatories.

⁂

I HAVE BEEN ASKED TO DISCUSS juvenile delinquency prevention in a community. This is a very complex problem which faces every hamlet, village, and town, of our great nation. Two hundred thousand youths are being arrested annually in this country. Countless dollars are being spent to eliminate juvenile delinquency but to no avail.

The juvenile court, which a generation ago was greeted with much enthusiasm as a cure-all for juvenile delinquency,

Speech by Father Edward J. Flanagan, National Conference of Catholic Charities, Chicago, Illinois, November 18, 1940, Girls and Boys Town Hall of History archives.

has utterly failed. True the juvenile court was intended as a step in the right direction by taking the young delinquent out of the adult court, separating him from the criminal in our jails, trying his case in a separate court which is supposed to assume a friendly attitude toward the child and help him instead of punish him. This child's court has proven ineffective for the reason that it has not the legal authority to establish a program by which this young delinquent can be thoroughly examined as to his physical, mental, and social and religious background. A program that approaches the child in a friendly and sympathetic manner. A program to solve the child's difficulty – not to punish him for his misdeeds – a program that will have a curative objective – not punitive. With children, the object must be to cure, not to punish.

The reformatories the nation over, instead of rehabilitating youth, actually have become schools of crime. Hardly a day goes by that we do not read in our newspapers of some young man being arrested for a crime and in the story it is noted that the boy had served one or two terms in some state reformatory.

In order to prevent delinquency in a community, we must understand thoroughly what causes this blight in our young and also its evidence.

What are these causes? The most important factor inducing delinquency is defective family relationships. The family is either the strongest barrier against delinquency or is a potent cause of delinquency. Children from lawless homes are often lawless. Children from homes in which trouble arises are often abused or neglected. Other causes include homes lacking economic security, homes where both parents are employed or where there is unemployment, and homes lacking cultural and religious stimulant. The crowded living conditions often drive children away from the homes and into delinquency. Improper movies, unfit literature, are also factors which lead children to delinquency.

What are our communities doing to counteract delinquency? As far as I can ascertain, this matter of delinquency is in the hands of the juvenile court and for the most part those who handle delinquents are of the politically minded type – unable to do anything except exact the pound of flesh in their program of punishment. There is no place in the juvenile court program for rehabilitation. Only by mere accident are some saved from wreckage. May I insert here, in justice to the fine men who preside on the benches of these courts throughout the country, that they realize how ineffective their program is and also how utterly helpless they are in promoting a program of rehabilitation under a Board of Commissioners who are politically minded men who believe in jail, prisons, and reform schools, but who will not spend a dollar to save a boy through other means.

In view of the fact that the youth of our nation is the backbone of our country and with souls precious in the sight of God, every effort should be taken to save these boys and girls. I say that every community should establish a social service bureau whose duties it would be to rehabilitate our youth.

In such a bureau, politics should be eliminated to the nth degree. Specialized workers should be in full charge of the program. The program should be based not upon punishment but on the philosophy of love, care, and kindness to youth.

It is through the social service that I see the solution of our youth problems of today. Every city establishing a social service bureau should have members on its board which would include a representative of the governing body of the city, the superintendent of the schools, the director of welfare, the chief of police, and the director of city recreation. Only through such a governing board as this can the problems which affect youth in general be coordinated.

With a social service bureau, delinquency can be very largely eliminated through scientific direction. It is the duty of each family to provide security, protection, and direction for their children but when the home fails it is necessary for the community to devise ways and means to prevent delinquency. This can be accomplished through this proposed social service bureau.

Every community owes an education to its children, this education to include religious training. It owes them the opportunities for healthy play and wholesome recreation. It also owes every child training in an occupation suited to his likes. It is the duty of every community to see that the proper handling of youth is maintained within its limits.

The school is an important agency in child training. The school has great responsibility in preparing children for good citizenship but our schools fail when they keep their doors open only from 8:00 until 3:30 in the afternoon. I say let us utilize these fine buildings and make them a part of our social service bureau set-up. I think it is ridiculous that school buildings costing hundreds of thousands of dollars are permitted to have their classrooms, gymnasiums, swimming pools, stand idle after school hours. After all, these school buildings belong to the people and they should be utilized as recreational and leisure time centers.

The police department naturally will play an important part in the social service bureau. In this new set-up, police must change the tactics that they have used in years gone by if this plan is to work. The policeman must realize that he is to help boys and prove to them that they are good boys and not have his heart set that every time he encounters a misguided youth the boy should be punished. The policeman must be willing to serve youth and take his reward in giving boys and girls a helping hand instead of seeking glory in arrest and convictions as reported on police bulletin boards and in newspapers.

Further, I would say that each police department should assign a certain number of picked men in plain clothes to work with juveniles exclusively, under the direction of this social service bureau. These men are to visit the homes of these boys from time to time and to seek out the causes of their misdeeds and work to an end of helping the boy, instead of carrying a club of punishment over his head. Juveniles should not be arrested and taken to any police stations, given rides in police cars, or permitted to be housed with criminals. Police should remember that a boy in mischief is a sick boy and should be taken, not to a police station, but to the headquarters of the social service bureau where a complete study of his case can be started and followed up.

Under such a plan full coordination of all public agencies would be inevitable. It is my opinion that in every city there is too much isolation between various units who rightfully are interested in youth. There is no coordination between these agencies. I refer to the schools, the police departments, the city government, and welfare agencies in general. It is my belief that too often individual units isolate themselves from other groups and work to the disadvantage of our youth, whereas, if they were united into one group, youth could be served instead of being penalized, as is now often the case.

It naturally follows that the social service board would need a guiding head, one who is a qualified worker in youth guidance, who could follow through the work of the board. This guiding head should be a psychologist if possible. I should also recommend a psychiatrist as a member of that board. It is possible that the school system could become the centralized agency from where the work could be directed, because the schools have the physical facilities for both recreational and educational activities and whatever expenses would be incurred would be negligible because of these existing facilities.

Here is how the social service bureau would operate. When a boy comes to the attention of either the school, the police, the welfare agency, or a private individual as being either delinquent or in danger of becoming a delinquent boy, the circumstances of the case would be reported to the bureau. The case-finding agency, be it either the school authorities or the police should make a report on the case to the bureau chief and not the juvenile court, as is now the case. General investigation should follow and a report made and discussed between the members of the bureau committee for their consideration. This investigation should include physical, mental, personality, social tests; a searching and comprehensive study of a child's relations to his home, school, church if any, neighborhood, associates; and other information which would be desirable to determine what type of supervision to be recommended in the boy's case.

Certainly after a case is thoroughly checked and constant follow-up made by either the investigating committee, plain clothes police officers, trained welfare workers, or school authorities, this program is bound to be successful. Of course, it will cost money, but even now thousands of dollars are being squandered in the manner in which we are handling juvenile delinquency through our juvenile courts and reformatory system. There is an old saying, "Crime does not pay," but the public is finally learning that it pays the crime bill in taxes. I am certain that under such a set-up as I have outlined here, the cost of rehabilitating youth will be greatly decreased. The emphasis will be placed on prevention and not upon punishment. This is our only salvation.

I have always contended that idleness is one of the great causes for delinquency. I am a firm believer that there is no such thing as a bad boy. I have studied several thousand cases of boys and I have never found one boy who wants to be bad. I am convinced that under the social service bureau an educational and recreational program can be planned and worked out which will embody boys and girls of all ages and that they will have little or no time available for idleness. The constructive program of education outside of the regular school day will have a broadening influence upon our youth as they will be given the opportunity for pursuit along leisure time activities such as woodcraft, photography, and so forth in addition to their recreational activities.

It is my opinion that such a plan should be instituted in every city or town of our nation. I am convinced that such a program must be instituted immediately. Let us save our youth from lives of crime. No boy is born bad but circumstances in his youth may direct him in the wrong direction. It is our duty to establish such bureaus of service and guidance which will rehabilitate those boys who have made a misstep in the early life. Let us eliminate misdeeds by establishing the proper guiding forces for our youth.

CHAPTER ELEVEN

A RESCUE MISSION ON THE HOME FRONT

To pursue his dream of entering the priesthood, Edward Flanagan, just turned eighteen, and his brother Patrick boarded the S.S. Celtic, sailing from Ireland to America in the late summer of 1904. One of their sisters had already made the ocean trip; their parents and all but two of seven other siblings would soon follow.

Flanagan was devoted to his new country and its ideals of democracy, equality, and government by the people. Those ideals were reflected in many aspects of his home for boys – the student-run government, the mixing of boys from all races and creeds, as well as the home's lack of fences and bars.

The advent of World War II created a frenzy of patriotic fervor on the Boys Town campus. Some of the older boys were allowed to enlist immediately, and the entire senior class of 1942 joined the armed forces after graduation. Flanagan became chaplain to "America's War Dads," and later, when hundreds of Boys Town alumni were serving in the military, he was named "Number One War Dad in America."

At the Home, Victory Gardens were planted and tons of scrap metal were collected for the war effort. Father Flanagan toured the coun-

try to speak at war bond rallies. During a one-week tour in November 1942, he sold nearly $3 million worth of bonds.

But Flanagan never lost the cadence of rural Ireland in his speech, and he never forgot his immigrant roots. With the same energy he exhibited in his efforts to support the war and American servicemen, he came to the passionate defense and rescue of an immigrant group caught in the crossfire of wartime emotion – the Japanese-Americans.

"To be an American," he said in a radio speech before the war, "means that I will be found always on the side of every man who is oppressed, and always the relentless foe of the oppression, regardless of what form it may assume. It means that I will expose fraud and deceit without fear or favoritism. It means that in my own efforts to protect my own rights I will never be found guilty of trampling on the rights and privileges of my fellow citizen."

Author James Ivey tells the story of how the Japanese-Americans came to Boys Town.

⚹⚹

THE TALL GANGLY PRIEST STRODE across the floor of the Midwestern railroad terminal, adjusting his glasses and smiling as he looked over the odd company before him: a Japanese-American mother with a baby in her arms, two small daughters at her side, and a Japanese-American man behind.

The meeting in the soft September 1942 night was the first between the James Takahashi family, Katsu Okida, and Father

By James Ivey, Copyright © Father Flanagan's Boys' Home.

Edward J. Flanagan. Far behind them, crossing the deserts of the republic, husband and father James Takahashi drove his pickup truck through the darkness to rejoin them, hoping this represented the end of what had been a nine-month nightmare.

The uncertainty in the party at the depot seemed to melt as the priest greeted them. Margaret Takahashi, in her reminiscence in the documentary book, *The Homefront,* recalled:

"I expected him to look like Spencer Tracy but he looked like Eddie Rickenbacker (the World War I air ace) ... when you first met him, you could feel this warmth. I've never felt that from another human being. He was so full of love that it radiated out from him. It was startling."

Then he produced what the oldest girl, Marilyn, who was called Winkie, thought was "the biggest paper bag I had ever seen." He proffered chocolate candies to the five-year-old Winkie and her younger sister, Leona.

That is how Winkie became a girl at Boys Town. She never forgot it.

"Those were the happiest days of my life," said the present Winkie, Mrs. Marilyn Fordney, a teacher and writer of textbooks near Oxnard, California.

The little party was the vanguard of an agonizing national migration that followed the Japanese bombing of Pearl Harbor on December 7, 1941. By February 18, 1942, President Franklin D. Roosevelt had signed Executive Order 9066. It permitted the government to remove certain peoples from certain areas – the Pacific Coast – for national defense and security.

In effect, it wrenched 120,000 Japanese-Americans from their California, Washington, and Oregon homes and moved them to the drylands of southeast Colorado, the swamps of Arkansas, and the cold, high plains in northern Wyoming. It collected them in fenced, hastily built, guarded communities remote from everyday life – America's concentration camps, historians quickly would label them.

The order also ripped up the rights of 77,000 of them, for they were American citizens born in this country – the Nisei. The order did not distinguish between the Issei, born in Japan, and their sons and daughters who were born here.

In the camps they were sent to, people would be born and die. Sons would go into the Army and serve their country. Some would be killed in battle while their country held their parents and brothers and sisters behind barbed wire with guns trained on them.

Most of the Japanese-Americans who pursued that 20th Century trail of tears have no difficulty recalling how it started. On that warm Sunday afternoon late in 1941, strange sights and sounds confronted the 2,000 Japanese-American residents of Terminal Island. Trucks and lorries bearing troops bustled along the island near Long Beach, California; soldiers swarmed the gantries and cranes of the maritime center, and plain-clothed Federal Bureau of Investigation agents rounded up many.

Most residents picked up were Issei born in Japan. They were aliens, California law having prohibited Japan-born residents from becoming citizens for thirty-five years.

An island Japanese-American doctor and his wife had a visitor that day, Lily Okura. She and husband Pat had been married only a few months. Pat Okura, who received a master's degree from UCLA in 1935, was in administration for the City of Los Angeles. All were Nisei, born in the U.S.

Pat was playing golf with Lily's father at Lakewood County Club in Long Beach that day. It was one of the few clubs that permitted use by Japanese-Americans.

As activity mounted on the island, considered a sensitive naval placement, her hosts decided they should return Lily to the mainland. The doctor later recalled how difficult that once-simple task became. The ferry to the island was not operating. The bridge had been closed.

When the party stopped to inquire how Mrs. Okura could be returned, they were taken into an office, fingerprinted and photographed. Fishermen from the island's fishing fleet encountering the same experience saw them and called, "Look, they got the doctor, too."

Lily Okura didn't get home until nearly midnight. The day and the troubles that followed were times not to be forgotten by the Okuras, who now direct the Okura Mental Health Leadership Foundation out of Bethesda, Maryland.

Another Nisei, Peter Okada, now a retired importer-exporter in Kirkland, Washington, also remembers. Then living with his widowed mother near Los Angeles, he had gone fishing along the coast that day. The bizarre spectacle of soldiers pulling cannon into a near-by tomato field interrupted the idyllic venture.

He decided to go home. On the way, people glared and scowled and shouted things at him.

Okada also remembers one of the Terminal Island fishermen, Katsu Okida, a carpenter on a trawler who helped a brother on an ice truck between fishing trips. Okida was "a very industrious and talented man in very many ways," according to Okada.

Okida would leave the island in the next few days and would not return to his home for over two years. He would go back mainly to inspect damage done there by vandals. A few months later, he would be killed in the service of the country that had evicted him and imprisoned his parents.

The events of the day, December 7, 1941, uprooted the lives of all of these people. The next day, the United States would be at war with Japan, Germany, and Italy.

Not far inland, James and Margaret Takahashi worried over the news. They were expecting their third child and James was going to school while starting a nursery of rare plants. Margaret had special problems. Her mother had been Irish, her father Japanese-American. By fate, she was born during a visit to Japan, so was not and could not be a U.S. citizen, but "we didn't feel Japanese. We felt American. That was the way we were raised."

The heart-searing events would leave 120,000 Japanese-Americans with no choice. They would be swept away from coastal homes to cold and unfriendly camps in the innards of America. But the Okuras and Okada, the Takahashis and Katsu Okida and many others would discover an option in the form of the tall Irish-American priest at Boys Town in a place that sounded like a Japanese city – Omaha.

Executive Order 9066, backed by West Coast politicians, pressure groups and frequently hysterical newspapers, was implemented by Lt. Gen. John DeWitt, often the focus of criticism. At one point, he also spoke of removing German- and Italian-born residents but this was shouted down.

The FBI's J. Edgar Hoover ridiculed the "hysteria and lack of judgment" of DeWitt's intelligence division and the famous Gen. Joseph W. (Vinegar Joe) Stilwell wrote simply in his notes that DeWitt was "a jackass." Asked once about the fact that no local Japanese-Americans had committed any hostile acts, DeWitt performed some semantic gymnastics: "The very fact that no sabotage has taken place is a disturbing and confirming indication that such action will be taken."

The camps were to be months in the building. In the meantime, DeWitt ordered the coastal Japanese-Americans interned at temporary places, usually racetracks. Japanese-Americans in the Los Angeles area were given from forty-eight hours – at Terminal Island – to two weeks to sell or rent homes and businesses before they were taken to the Santa Anita Race Track.

They could take only what they could carry. Caucasian mates followed husbands and wives through the camps.

It was at Santa Anita that many made the connection with Father Flanagan through one of the camp administrators, E. J. England, and his secretary, Lily Okura. England, a Notre Dame graduate, knew Father Hugh Lavery, superior at the Maryknoll Japanese Catholic Center in Los Angeles. Maryknoll at the time operated an orphanage, and Father Flanagan and Father Lavery had exchanged information on philosophies and methods.

England "was a very compassionate man," the Okuras remember, and many Japanese-Americans had gone to the Maryknoll School. Thus a message from Father Flanagan was passed on to England and then Mrs. Okura: Boys Town had a manpower shortage because of the war. It would be willing to make places for some Japanese-Americans if they fit Boys Town needs.

This, Okura said, was nearly two years before the U.S. government, realizing its need for more labor, began releasing Nisei for work over the nation.

"Father Flanagan was two years ahead of his time," Pat Okura said.

Directly or indirectly through this connection, Okura estimates that about three hundred Japanese-Americans found their way to Boys Town and the vicinity for at least part of the next three years. Most passed on to jobs and lives in other regions.

Boys Town records show ten Japanese-Americans were working there by April 1943. Through the end of the war, a total of forty-two actually lived and worked at Boys Town. Father Flanagan frequently paid for transportation to the Omaha area, provided work and a paycheck, and scouted up lodging, either at Boys Town or nearby. Boys Town officials also found jobs for others in neighboring cities.

"He was the anchor for us," said Okura. "It (going to Boys Town) changed my life. I don't know today what would have happened. Not too many people know what he did here. He was a man of strong convictions, and he thought what was happening to us was wrong. He was determined to do whatever he could to help. What a great humanitarian he was."

The interlude between Pearl Harbor and their removal to the assembly centers had not been kind to Okura and other

Nisei. Bank accounts were frozen. Nisei who had been classified as A1 in the draft now found themselves reclassified as aliens.

Okura was the first Japanese-American hired by the City of Los Angeles and by 1941, about fifty were on the payroll, most of them secretaries and clerks. Okura, who was doing technical research for setting up a new personnel and examination system, found himself under attack by news media. In one broadcast, he was accused of infiltrating the city with Japanese-Americans to sabotage the water and power supplies.

Angry and hurt, Okura said when he first went to Santa Anita, "I decided I wouldn't lift a finger."

Then, when his wife found out about Boys Town, he decided he would help out by volunteering to aid in removal to permanent camps. The act made the Okuras the last to leave Santa Anita, in the fall of 1942. They were boarding for one of the camps when an eleventh hour incident changed all.

Japanese-Americans could leave custody only for a few hours. To be gone longer, they needed a special pass. The Okuras had a letter of acceptance from Boys Town as the fall wore on – but no travel pass.

"On the day we were to leave for Arkansas, this soldier came through, looking for an Irishman named Pat 'O'Kura.' He had the pass for us," Okura recalled.

Okura, who came to Boys Town as a psychologist, was to remain in the area for more than twenty-five years, working out of the juvenile court, then the Nebraska Psychiatric Institute before moving to Washington with the National Institute of Mental Health in 1970. He is now retired.

Peter Okada heard about Boys Town from Lily Okura and wrote to Father Flanagan. He was moved to the Amache Camp at Granada, Colorado, before he received word from Boys Town and got a travel pass.

Of those days and Father Flanagan's intervention, he said:

"I think he believed the internment was wrong but he was just an Irish priest. So he decided to help out any way he could, to rectify the wrong and still support his country. He was a great man."

Okada remembers his year at Boys Town as "one of the best years of my life. They treated me so well," he said. "I left a younger brother behind at the relocation camp, and I was concerned about him. When I told Father Flanagan about it, he asked me why I hadn't said something about it earlier. He told me to send for him and I did. My younger brother ended up graduating from Boys Town High School."

The Takahashis, with their newest child, son James, were preparing to go to Amache in September when their pass came through. Father Flanagan encouraged them to bring their truck: it could be used in his job as supervisor of the grounds. That is why Margaret and the children traveled across the country on a train with Katsu Okida, James far behind in the truck.

"My husband wrote him a letter and he wrote back right away and told us to come. That was Father Flanagan's mission – to take the rejected or unwanted," Mrs. Takahashi later said.

Katsu Okida also had written to Father Flanagan. His letter still is in the home's old files. The last line reads: "Even if I cannot go, it is certainly heartening to know of someone who has taken an interest in these trying times."

While James took care of the lawn and gardens, his family moved into an old farmhouse a half-mile east of Boys Town. Mrs. Takahashi learned to can and to cook on a wood stove. Winkie went to a one-room country school. They had friends who were German, Italian, all nationalities. "They didn't care what nationality we were," remembered James Takahashi just before his death a few years ago.

In 1944, when the U.S. armed forces began again accepting Japanese-Americans, both Okada and Okida enlisted.

Okada received special training and was assigned to aid occupational forces in the Far East. He was to see Father Flanagan one more time: during the priest's trip to assist his country in re-establishing home and family life in Japan and Korea.

The press at Kyoto, Japan, recorded a dramatic meeting between the two in April 1947, as the two discussed old times at Boys Town.

Okada, who came to Boys Town as a gardener and driver, was witness to a famous Flanagan incident and on that occasion, recalled it for the press. He had been driving the priest to Omaha when they saw two boys obviously from the home. They picked the pair up, and, during the short ride, Father Flanagan mentioned everything but running away. Then they stopped for an ice cream soda and the priest softly asked: "What did we do to make you want to run away?"

Heads down, the two said they would never leave again.

Father Flanagan interceded several times on behalf of Japanese-Americans in their troubles with the establishment. One case, that of Kazue Oda Takahashi (no relation to the

James Takahashis), occupied much of the last three years of the priest's life.

Paul Takahashi was a Nisei, a barber who came early to Boys Town with a new family. His first wife had died several years before. In 1937, during a trip to Japan, he met Kazue, a teacher. They married and she came to the United States. After coming to Boys Town, they learned that the government intended to deport Kazue as an alien, forcing her also to take two young children with her into exile.

Paul Takahashi's son by his first marriage, Tom, was entering the priesthood. In later recollections before his 1989 death, Father Takahashi reflected over bringing the deportation letter to Father Flanagan for advice.

"As he was reading, his anger rose," the Japanese-American priest wrote.

Then Father Flanagan called the head of the U.S. Department of Justice. Mrs. Takahashi was given a temporary stay while Father Flanagan launched a series of letters to Congressmen and immigration officials.

Cutting through the red tape of the bureaucracy, in 1946, Father Flanagan wrote officials that Mrs. Takahashi was "caught in the net of war, intrigue, enmity, malignity and punishment ... there must be in this great Christian country of ours an interpretation of law which would exclude such cruel separation as this order would compel."

Finally, in April 1948, a month before Father Flanagan's death, Mrs. Takahashi was the subject of a Congressional relief act, which permitted her to stay. Tom Takahashi said his family had received much from Father Flanagan and Boys Town, "materially and spiritually."

Katsu Okida landed in the 442nd Regimental Combat Team, the Japanese-American unit that was the most decorated military organization in World War II – and had the highest casualties.

In November 1944, Father Flanagan wrote to inquire of Katsu about Pat Okura's brother, Susuma (Babe) who was killed in France. The Boys Town director concluded his letter:

"Be assured, Kat, that I remember you very dearly in my humble prayers, as I do all my boys. You are one of us and we shall not forget you."

It never got to his friend. In December, the Okida family wrote:

"Dear Father Flanagan:

We have just received news from the War Department that Katsu was killed in action on November 6 in France. That Katsu was baptized before going overseas is a special consolation for all of us.

From his letters we knew that he had truly found God and we are most deeply grateful to you, dear Father, for you were indeed inspiring to Katsu and helped make his way to God. Our sincerest thanks for all you have done for Katsu."

By 1947, the James Takahashis were on their way back to California: "I just loved it there (at Boys Town), I didn't want to come back but my husband wanted to be his own boss," Margaret Takahashi wrote.

Pat Okura considers himself one of the lucky ones. The family had rented their floral shop to a stranger when they were forced to leave Los Angeles. The occupants took good care of the property and gave it back promptly after the war, he said.

Not so lucky for the Okadas. Peter said the family had to go to court for several months to get their home back.

The times are still remembered at the Maryknoll Japanese Catholic Center in the old Little Tokyo area east of Los Angeles City Hall. About 3,000 parishioners, most of them Japanese-American, worship at the four-building complex. Ask them about Father Flanagan and Japanese-Americans and they probably will say oh, yes, this is familiar.

Harry Honda has been a Japanese-American newsman around Los Angeles for more than forty years. Now editor emeritus of the *Pacific Citizen* and historian for Maryknoll, he said what Boys Town became for the besieged Japanese-Americans has not been forgotten.

"It has been passed on by word of mouth for generations," said Honda. "They have very positive thoughts about Boys Town and Father Flanagan."

CHAPTER TWELVE

 # THE IRISH INDUSTRIAL SCHOOLS

When Father Flanagan was invited on a speaking tour of his native Ireland in 1946, he agreed to go but carried with him a second, hidden agenda. He had received correspondence from political reformers, parents, and former residents of Ireland's industrial schools asking him to look into the reportedly harsh conditions at the schools. What he discovered at these schools appalled him, and he candidly criticized them both during his trip and on his return. In a school in Belfast, he witnessed a large group of children under eleven years old making shoes in a windowless basement room lit by a single bulb.

His controversial visit, not appreciated by many in Ireland, is recounted in the book, "Suffer the Little Children: The Inside Story of Ireland's Industrial Schools," by Mary Raftery and Eoin O'Sullivan. Father Flanagan's criticisms were repudiated by Irish officials, and not until 1970 did a public investigation finally reveal the widespread malnutrition, child labor, and physical and sexual abuse that existed in these schools.

IN 1946, THOSE RUNNING INDUSTRIAL schools in Ireland were to receive a most unpleasant shock. They were subjected to unprecedented public criticism, and from one of their own – a priest.

Monsignor Edward Flanagan's visit to Ireland in 1946 was something of a milestone for the country. Feted wherever he went, he attracted large crowds to his public meetings. He was treated like a film star, and indeed he was the next best thing – a hit Hollywood movie had been made about his life and work.

Boys Town, which opened in 1939, featured Spencer Tracy and Mickey Rooney, two of Hollywood's biggest stars at the time. The film was hugely popular, particularly in Ireland, and Spencer Tracy won a Best Actor Oscar for his portrayal of Fr. Flanagan.

The movie told the story of the founding of Boys Town in Nebraska, a residential child care centre catering for boys of all creeds and colours. Fr. Flanagan had battled against the odds to open this centre, which received no financial support from the US Government.

Though in fact Irish, from Ballymoe in Co. Galway, Fr. Flanagan had spent all his adult life in the United States, working with homeless and delinquent boys. He was an enlightened priest, far ahead of his time in terms of his approach to child care. His slogan – "There's no such thing as a bad boy" –

From *Suffer the Little Children: The Inside Story of Ireland's Industrial Schools*, by Mary Raftery and Eoin O'Sullivan, Copyright © 1999, pgs. 189-195. Reprinted by permission of The Continuum International Publishing Group, Inc., New York.

summed up the policy of Boys Town, where physical punishment of the children was not permitted.

Fr. Flanagan was horrified to discover the widespread use of severe physical punishment in industrial and reformatory schools (and in prisons) in Ireland. In a statement issued to the press at the end of his visit to Ireland in July 1946, he described these institutions as "a disgrace to the nation."[1]

He had given a series of public lectures in cities around the country. His packed audiences invariably included senior members of the Catholic Church. In Limerick and Waterford, for example, the local bishops were in attendance.

He used the opportunities provided to elaborate on his own child care philosophy – to love, support and encourage the children in his care. But he also contrasted the approach of Boys Town USA to the attitudes towards children in care in Ireland. Addressing a packed audience at the Savoy Cinema in Cork, he stated: "You are the people who permit your children and the children of your communities to go to these institutions of punishment. You can do something about it, first by keeping your children away from these institutions." These remarks brought prolonged applause from the audience.

The Irish Government, however, was not quite so ecstatic about Fr. Flanagan's criticisms of its child care institutions. Fianna Fail's Gerry Boland, the then Minister for Justice, responded angrily. In Dail Eireann, on 23rd of July 1946, he accused Fr. Flanagan of using "offensive and intemperate language" concerning "conditions about which he has no firsthand knowledge."

Sean Brady TD asked the Minister if he was aware of American press reports that Fr. Flanagan had stated that "physical punishment, including the cat-o'-nine tails, the rod, and fist, is used in reform schools both here and in Northern Ireland."

Minister Boland answered that he was indeed aware of these statements. "I was not disposed to take any notice of what Mgr. Flanagan said while he was in this country because his statements were so exaggerated that I did not think that people would attach any importance to them. When, however, on his return to America, he continued to make statements of this kind, I feel it is time that someone should reply."

It is a somewhat telling point that the Government only felt the need to respond to Fr. Flanagan's very serious criticisms of its institutions when that criticism was given coverage outside of the country.

In fact, the American coverage of the controversy was a source of great outrage to James Dillon TD, later the leader of Fine Gael. He referred in the Dail to how "Monsignor Flanagan turned up in this country and went galumphing around … got his photograph taken a great many times and made a variety of speeches to tell us what a wonderful man he was and of the marvels he had achieved in the United States. He then went back to America and published a series of falsehoods and slanders."

The Ceann Comhairle interrupted at this point: "That is rather severe language."

Unabashed, Dillon continued: "when a Catholic Monsignor uses language which appears to give the colour of justification to cartoons in American papers where muscular warders are flogging half-naked fourteen-year-old boys with cats-of-nine-tails, I think it is right to say in public of that Monsignor that he should examine his conscience and ask himself if he has spoken the truth ... If he finds that the substance of what he is alleged to have said is grossly untrue, then he should have the moral courage to come out in public. and say so, and correct in so far as he can, the grave injustice he has done not only to the legislators of this country; but to the decent, respectable, honest men who are members of the Irish Christian Brothers."

When Fr. Flanagan replied to these attacks, the issue turned into a substantial controversy. "As a result of my denouncement of the penal institutions in Ireland," stated Fr. Flanagan, "I have made statements that caused the people in authority to feel rather uncomfortable." While in Ireland, he said, he had in fact visited several reform schools and prisons. He had also paid a visit to Artane Industrial School, often described as Ireland's Boys Town.

Fr. Flanagan also stated that the use in these institutions of "severe physical punishment for the inmates is hardly in keeping with the high ideals of a Christian nation. ... I do not believe that a child can be reformed by lock and key and bars, or that fear can ever develop a child's character. ... If trying to help the forgotten boys of reform schools and prisons, whether it be in Ireland or in the United States, is intemperate and offensive, I'm afraid I'll have to plead guilty."

A vigorous correspondence on the issue continued for several months in the letters pages of several newspapers. Most of the letters were favourable to Fr. Flanagan. However, there were several more traditional views expressed. P. O'Reilly, for example, wrote the following to the *Times Pictorial* of 7th September 1946: "Through original sin children are naturally vicious little savages, and it needs a rigorous discipline with fear as a wholesome deterrent to mould them into decent citizens."

The following week, also in the *Times Pictorial*, T.R. Kearney violently disagreed with this view. Calling P. O'Reilly "a particularly disgusting type of prig," he went on to condemn his letter as bearing "the stamp of a bigoted lout, and that judging by the opinions expressed therein, the only youthful being which could, with benefit to itself, be entrusted to his care is a baby gorilla."

Even such luminaries as Maud Gonne MacBride contributed to the exchange of letters, although hers (to the *Times Pictorial* on 12th October 1946) was mainly confined to the poor conditions in Irish prisons. She did however add: "One would like to know more of actual conditions in the borstals, reformatories and industrial schools to which these juveniles are being sent, for the 'Father of Boystown' warns us that some of these institutions are unsatisfactory and need to be changed."

However, the tide appeared to turn in the Government's favour when the Irish Press printed an editorial on the controversy (16th October, 1946). That paper accused Fr. Flanagan of having behaved "in an entirely irresponsible manner." His criticisms, the paper said, were based on hearsay only, and were "so reckless and so far removed from the truth that nobody in this country is likely to pay much attention to them."

In private correspondence during February 1947 to one of his many friends in Ireland, Fr. Flanagan wrote: "I am not sorry that I have opened up this discussion. It seems that people over there are afraid to come out and discuss things in which the government has something to say, because of fear."

In private, he was also far more direct about the nature of the Irish industrial schools system, describing it in February 1947:

> ... the institutionalization of little children, housed in great big factory-like places, where individuality has been, and is being, snuffed out with no development of the personality ... and where little children become a great army of child slavery in workshops, making money for the institutions which give them a little food, a little clothing, very little recreation and a doubtful education.
>
> How can those people become inspired with religion when they think with their more adult minds back over the years where they had been child laborers? ... How in the name of God could a man like Mr. Boland (the then Minister for Justice) justify his stewardship of these helpless little children throughout the little island of Eire when he is face to face with all the information that has come out through the papers since last July – criticisms which I so justly made. All he has done is deny them and try to put me in a bad light with the church and otherwise by trying to strike at my character.

Fr. Flanagan's views on the Irish hierarchy and its role in child care are interesting. Once again in private correspondence he wrote in 1947: "Since nearly all of the [Irish] people are Catholic, the hierarchy has to be very careful not to offend the people in power. ... But the church should protect the welfare of these children. It should keep a vigilant eye on those who are in charge of these institutions and should visit them most frequently and not make these visits occasions of wining and dining."

At this stage, Fr. Flanagan had been provided with very detailed information on the beating of a boy by Christian Brothers in Glin Industrial School in Co. Limerick – this boy, still bearing the marks of the whip on his back "was one of the few to escape after such beatings so that their mistreatment might be exposed." ... Flanagan had made a brief reference to this case in one of his public statements, and it had given rise to the cartoon in *American Weekly* of a grotesque cleric beating a small boy, so vividly described in Dail Eireann by James Dillon.

Fr. Flanagan appeared to have held rather a dim view of the Christian Brothers for some time. Again in private correspondence he writes:

> We have no Christian Brotherhood here at Boys Town. We did have them for five years but they left after they found out that they could not punish the children and kick them around. ...
>
> Your great country that is sending forth missionaries into foreign lands ... might well learn to begin at home to do a little missionary work among the unwanted, unloved, untrained and unfed children, who are suppressed and have become slaves because

of the dictatorial policies of those in power. What you need over there is to have someone shake you loose from your smugness and satisfaction and set an example by punishing those who are guilty of cruelty, ignorance and neglect of their duties in high places. We have punished the Nazis for their sins against society. We have punished Fascists for the same reason. ... I wonder what God's judgment will be with reference to those who hold the deposit of faith and who fail in their God-given stewardship of little children?

What emerges so powerfully from Fr. Flanagan's private correspondence is his overwhelming sense of outrage at the mistreatment of children in industrial schools in Ireland. All of his life he spoke out passionately against the physical punishment of children. He perceived the beating of a child as being, without exception, destructive, and motivated by a combination of revenge and ignorance – "flogging and other forms of physical punishment wound that sense of dignity which attaches to the self. The result of such negative treatment is that the boy comes to look upon society as his enemy. His urge is to fight back."

Fr. Flanagan struggled with the difficulty of reconciling the Catholic nature of Irish society with apparent disregard for the conditions being endured by the children locked away in institutions. In a public statement in October 1946, he said that "the good people of Ireland can be trusted to do what Christian charity demands if they know the facts. The problem is to get the facts before them." However, four months later, in February

1947, he wrote sadly that "I don't seem to be able to understand the psychology of the Irish mind."

Fr. Flanagan was, however, determined not to give up. Throughout 1947 and into early 1948, he was preparing for a return visit to Ireland. This was in spite of his considerable international commitments – he had been appointed by President Harry S. Truman to advise on the needs of the world's homeless children in the aftermath of the Second World War, which involved him in extensive travel around the world.

In the middle of all this, he had already written to the Irish Government requesting permission to visit a substantial number of penal institutions for both adults and children in the country. He anticipated arriving in Ireland during the summer of 1948.

But he was never to make that visit. On the 13th of May 1948, during a field visit to Berlin and its homeless children, Fr. Flanagan suffered a major heart attack and died the next day. He was only sixty-one.

His untimely death effectively marked the end of this controversial public debate surrounding the care of children in industrial schools. Almost twenty years were to elapse before the issue once again came into the public arena. In that twenty years, roughly 15,000 children served out their time in industrial schools throughout the country, enduring conditions which had changed little from those condemned by Fr. Flanagan in 1946.

---

[1] All of the Fr. Flanagan material originates from the Boys Town Hall of History, Omaha, Nebraska, USA.

CHAPTER THIRTEEN

 # International Advocate for Children

At the end of World War II, President Harry Truman and the War Department asked Father Flanagan to undertake several trips to Asia and Europe to look into conditions faced by children who had been orphaned during the war. Plagued by bouts of ill health all his life, Flanagan suffered a heart attack on the last of these trips and died. Author James Ivey recounts his final mission on behalf of children.

᙭᙭

ON SATURDAY, MAY 15, 1948, the new State of Israel was one day old. That day, a race horse named Citation found only three other horses to compete against him and a man named Mel Patton ran one hundred yards faster than any man in history.

War-weary Americans were buying new cars and new homes. You could get a deluxe Ford coupe for $1,600 and a pretty swell nine-room house for about $9,000.

All this was far from the worried minds of the small group of men who scurried into the 279th Station Military Hospital in

Berlin behind the still figure on the stretcher. Inside, a quick diagnosis: heart attack. The patient was in critical condition. An Army chaplain was summoned. He delivered the sacraments shortly after 1 a.m. and the patient murmured, "Amen."

It was the last litany of the Rt. Rev. Msgr. Edward Joseph Flanagan – Father Flanagan, a title which had become more than religious appellation for thousands of boys. Death had come for the founder and only director of the esteemed Boys Town during a rigorous mission which once again underlined his belief there was no such thing as a bad boy.

International reaction came quickly, for the influence of the man who started with five boys on a hilltop corner in downtown Omaha three decades before now had fanned out far beyond the brick streets of that Midwest city or the rolling cornfields surrounding it.

He had been pursuing a solution for the Herculean problem of the homeless, rootless youth washed adrift by years of war.

And that quest during the last fifteen months of his life had taken him from shattered cities of Japan and Korea to behind the Iron Curtain, in Vienna, brushing shoulders and ideas with presidents and prelates, emperors, great generals and frustrated civilians, embittered students, ragged children, hard-eyed suspicious Communists.

A saddened President Truman, who had commissioned Father Flanagan to travel to Europe and advise what could be done to stabilize family-and-home structures, said the world's youth had lost "an everfaithful friend."

"He has left a living monument in the countless boys who are today honest men and upright citizens because of his benign influence and abiding faith in the inherent goodness of human nature," the President said.

The priest "died in the service of his country and all mankind," said Secretary of War Kenneth Royall of Father Flanagan's efforts to solve youth problems in strife-torn countries.

"No better man could have been chosen for work of this magnitude ... the results of his inspired labor will be far reaching and supremely significant," he said.

"He had the same impact on European youth as he did on us at Boys Town," said a former Boys Towner, Donald L. Roybal, now living in Palmerdale, Ala.

Roybal, then an Air Force staff sergeant who spent much of the last thirty days with the priest, said, "For kids there was an aura about him. They felt it when he came into a room."

In a twenty-four-inch story, the *New York Times* called him "a man of infinite capacity, moral courage and faith in God and youth." While a Catholic, it said, he made democracy the keynote at the most famous home for homeless boys and non-Catholics "are simply taught to believe in God and obey moral laws."

The call of the native-born Irishman's adopted land enjoined him to this whirlwind global tour in the last fifteen months of his life.

Americans were zooming back to the good life as fast as they had plunged into war six years before. The big movie popular in 1947 even proclaimed, *"It's a Wonderful Life."*

That was not the image confronting Father Flanagan early in 1947 with the message from the U.S. government, initialed by General Douglas MacArthur. It requested the priest's services on a trip to the Far East to advise the Japanese government on welfare programs and youth troubles.

In many lands, homes were shattered, families scattered, youth at risk. It asked Father Flanagan to give "special emphasis" on the care of abandoned and orphaned children.

The sixty-day grind began on a transport ship headed for Tokyo.

Between April 24 and June 23, 1947, Father Flanagan visited sixteen Japanese and South Korean cities, conducting large mass public meetings in each with MacArthur and Japanese leaders. He talked with residents of forty-eight orphanages, shelters, reformatories and refugee centers.

His investigations took him far from the beaten track: into the underground railways and stations of Japan, dark and sinister in the cold aftermath of war. These had been nocturnal shelters for homeless waifs of the cities.

He complimented authorities on their recovery efforts but called for a national survey to determine the actual number of homeless youths.

Japan always had a strong family tradition, he noted, but for thousands, war had destroyed this and the country had no significant foster home system. Youngsters ran away from temporary homes because food was bad, conditions were poor and frequently unsanitary, medical attention usually was non-existent. Because of the previous strong family ties, Father Flanagan observed that detention for homeless Japanese children was "very foreign."

Now children ran the streets, stealing and begging, a shock to older Japanese. Often they lived in the underground railways. With an interpreter, Father Flanagan poked into the stations nightly, talking with the children, hearing their complaints, investigating them.

He learned of "homes" that actually were sweat shops in which young boys worked long hours six days a week – in one ages were from eight to fourteen. Father Flanagan condemned them and found it deplorable that the products of their labor were sold for profit with the gains "not being returned for the benefit of the children within the institution."

South Korea, he said, suffered from the "saddest circumstances of any liberated country in the world today ... there is no time for childhood in Korea. The transition from babyhood into mature endeavor is not distinguishable."

It distressed him: because they were expected to contribute to the family budget, "the children do not play in Korea like the children in other countries."

He criticized such practices as housing boys and girls together and placing new orphanage inmates into solitary confinement for several days upon arrival.

His report, "Children of Defeat," was presented to President Truman in Washington at a meeting July 7. He "heartily recommended" a foster home system and said that because of Japanese inexperience in dealing with homeless children it was necessary for Occupation Forces "to orient the Japanese people on the need for these homes for Japanese children."

Better living and health conditions and gender separation were urged. He called for tighter regulation of orphanages "to make racketeering impossible behind the guise of aiding help-less, starving little children."

Father Flanagan was only back a few months when President Truman, impressed by the Oriental project, asked him to make a similar fact-finding mission to war-torn Europe.

The priest had not been a robust person since childhood illnesses in Ireland and he privately confided to friends about another fatiguing journey – but he agreed. He attacked the new appointment with as much vigor and intensity as the first. This time with Patrick Norton, Boys Town general manager and his nephew, as diarist, he left New York City by ship March 5, 1948, arriving in Vienna by train March 11.

Father Flanagan encountered Communist antagonism to religion there and commented, "In Japan, the life has not been destroyed as it has been in Austria."

Traveling thousands of miles through Central Europe in drafty military propeller-driven airplanes or vehicles and the continent's rebuilding railroads, he found an estimated 40,000 children in the Vienna area were designated as homeless and in poor shape physically and emotionally.

He called for more playgrounds and sports, saying it was better than the saloons and brothels which now drew youth.

He espoused for Europe an idea advanced for that time: daylong kindergartens to help out the army of single mothers who had to work.

Still driving himself, he gave the Easter Mass in Vienna that day. A few hours later, the priest collapsed. Doctors were called and electrocardiographs were taken. They found his circulation poor but nothing else wrong and urged him to slow down.

But by April 3, he was traveling again. With him now was Roybal, one of several boys Father Flanagan and Norton met in Europe. Roybal had taken thirty days of leave from his post with the staff of an Army-formed Boys Town at Buchhof, Germany. He still remembers it.

"We were in an orphanage in Vienna. He was already tired and as we were climbing up to the third floor, well, he just got all tuckered out. We had to help him up and at the top, he sent us on ahead."

"I can't let the boys see me like this," he told Norton and Roybal.

"A couple of minutes later he came on in, all smiles, as if nothing had happened. He wouldn't slow down," said Roybal.

On April 25, he visited his old college rooms at Innsbruck. He stayed a night in Heidelberg, then traveled to West Berlin. The conferences and the planning for his recommendations frequently kept Father Flanagan up until midnight, night after night.

On May 14, following a visit to Hamburg, he flew once again to Berlin. On the flight, an engine cut out and they limped in on one motor, an hour late, emergency equipment standing by.

After a meeting with representatives of Gen. Lucius D. Clay, the pace didn't slacken. At 2 p.m. they were at a German youth center for conferences, learned West Berlin alone had 10,000 homeless youth. The center had fed 76,000 at Christmas.

At a reception that evening, Father Flanagan met with an old Innsbruck college classmate, Conrad Cardinal von Preysing of Berlin. Then the priest and Norton retired to Harnoch Haus, discussing recommendations he planned to make to General Clay, military governor of Germany, the next day.

He decided he would talk about youth border crossings and a lack of supervision. He would suggest closer relationships between churches of West Berlin, the Berlin Youth Administration and the military government. Occupation forces should supply welfare workers for youth centers but adult leadership should be provided by German people – Germans, he said, best understood their own children.

The recommendations were never made by Father Flanagan. After midnight May 15, Norton wrote that he heard a knock at his door. The priest was there.

"Pat, I have a pain in my chest. Please get a doctor right away," he said.

A doctor was called. He ordered the priest to the station hospital. Despite feverish efforts, last sacraments were given about 1 a.m. by the chaplain, Capt. Emmett L. Walsh. Through his final conversations, Chaplain Walsh wrote later, he "talked very natural-like," several times stroking his heavy eyebrows, a characteristic. He died shortly after 2 a.m. – "a beautiful and peaceful death," the chaplain recalled.

Shock waves rippled both the military establishment in Berlin and back in America, where at Boys Town several said they felt they had lost a father for the second time.

In accordance with one of the priest's last requests, Norton the next day passed on verbally to Clay Father Flanagan's observations about German youth problems. A formal report to the President was made by Norton a month later.

The task of preparing for Father Flanagan's last trip home began with a Mass the following Monday in Berlin, attended by thousands. Then the long, sorrowing flight began, from Berlin through the Azore Islands to Smoky Hills Air Base in Kansas and finally, to Omaha.

More than 1,500 met the plane and followed it west out from the city, passing the downtown summit where Father Flanagan had established his first boys' home.

Because of the crowds, two services were held at Boys Town. The Rev. Edmond C. Walsh, acting Boys Town director, called Father Flanagan's death "the end of a great and glorious journey."

He preached from the Book of Matthew: "I was a stranger and you took me in."

The great humanitarian was buried in a corner at the Boys Town chapel. A few days later, President Truman visited Boys Town to lay a wreath at his tomb and receive a final report of the mission.

Within a week more than 5,400 messages and prayers had been received from around the world. They came from religious and government leaders over the world, from entertainment and sports figures, from Spencer Tracy, the great actor who played Father Flanagan in films, from makers of *Boys Town*, from Congressmen and newsboys, from just plain people.

Japanese Welfare Director Giichi Taketa, said new child welfare laws based on Father Flanagan's recommendations were being approved and "it is our great sorrow to hear this sad news before the happy reports … could reach him."

Within a year, eighty-nine Boys Towns or homes patterned after Boys Town had been established. As the world recovered and needs changed or diminished, most of the homes disappeared or consolidated with other organizations.

Still going is the oldest, at Engadine, New South Wales, Australia, founded before the war after a priest, Thomas V. Dunlea, saw the movie, *Boys Town*, and communicated with Father Flanagan.

Also functioning are Boys Town programs in Italy, Israel, Japan, South Africa, and Korea.

Father Flanagan's reports of his fifteen-month pilgrimage may be only a token of its importance. Perhaps more significant was what he did, his personal contacts.

A poignant remembrance of it still is in the files at Boys Town, an aged envelope bearing a hand-written letter and some small, yellowing box camera photos of Father Flanagan among Japanese boys and girls. Incorrectly routed in mailing, it arrived after the services. It is from the Hiroshima War Orphanage. The eighty-five children there lost parents in the bomb blast.

The children had held services with Father Flanagan at a church in Hiroshima during the 1947 visit, when the pictures were taken. They returned sadly to the same church a year later for services after his death.

"In Japan, when the sweet-scent of early summer is being felt, we heard that our respected and loved Father Edward J.

Flanagan had died of a heart attack at Berlin unexpectedly … it is a great sad information," the letter begins.

"We remember clearly that smile like Papa on his face. Father Flanagan was the star and father of all the world boys. His body is dead but his spirit is alive in our Japanese boys breathe (sic).

"We pray for the repose of Father Flanagan's soul."

CHAPTER FOURTEEN

'A Good Man of God'

As word of Father Flanagan's death spread, condolences and tributes poured into Boys Town. Former residents, current boys, and staff, as recounted in James Ivey's account below, were especially shocked and saddened to lose so suddenly the founder whose faith and love had been their guiding beacon for more than thirty years.

Rabbi Edgar F. Magnin's eulogy of Father Flanagan in The Los Angeles Times reflected the thoughts of many: "The world is poorer today for his passing, but the angels are richer and rejoice in his coming. Indeed, the world is richer in another sense than it was before he entered it, for he will live on in the hearts and minds of Americans in ages yet to come. The setting sun always leaves a trail of glory long after it has bowed its way out in the West and the arms of night have enfolded themselves around the earth."

IT IS A HUMAN MANIFESTATION that where we were, what we were doing, is imprinted on our minds when a marked moment in life transpires. So it is that one of the occupants of the car traveling west on the two-lane highway near Dubuque, Iowa, vividly remembers that May 15, 1948, morning when the announcer on the car radio read the bulletin: Boys Town's Father Edward J. Flanagan was dead of a heart attack in Berlin, Germany.

The car slowed down sharply. Inside were the Rev. Peter Dunne, a Boys Town dean, and the Rt. Rev. Msgr. Francis Schmitt, then the director of the famous Boys Choir.

"We were shocked. We couldn't say anything. We just pulled over to the side of the road and prayed," recalled Father Dunne, the last priest of Father Flanagan's still on the Boys Town staff.

"I remembered the last time talking to him, just before he left for Europe. We were looking out over the new cottages being built, the biggest project we had. He was looking forward to opening them," said Father Dunne.

Most of the world sees Father Flanagan as a man of dogged perseverance and boundless energy who took his feeling for fellow man, an idea and, step-by-step, framed out and built the most noted boys home in the world.

Father Dunne also sees him steeped in spirituality. As a result, he said, Father Flanagan often talked of taking up the rigors and spiritual solitude of the monastic life when he felt his Boys Town work was finished.

"If he felt he ever had this mission solidified, he said he would become a Trappist monk. I think he would have. He felt a deep relationship with the Lord and deeply involved himself daily in prayer," he said.

By James Ivey, Copyright © Father Flanagan's Boys' Home.

Father Dunne, a native Omahan, found this consecration and devotion obvious in 1944 when, as a twenty-five year old, his first assignment after seminary was at Boys Town. When he was summoned to Boys Town, he was "amazed and happy. I wasn't expecting it."

"I would have the opportunity to work with Father Flanagan. It was overwhelming," he said.

He quickly found out that the priest maintained a monastic schedule at the center. Divine offices including recitation of scriptures and a spiritual reading and prayer began the day at 6 a.m.

"No one got to the chapel before Father Flanagan," said Father Dunne.

"He enjoyed prayer. He felt a contemplative life strengthened what was already there."

Similar liturgy followed every noon and evening meal, a schedule similar to those in monasteries.

Following the divine offices, the staff met with the director to talk over events of the day. The staff then would retire, he said, "but Father Flanagan usually was off again to meet with someone else. He was a whirlwind of activity."

An acuteness to humanity in Father Flanagan permitted him to see the problems about him, said Father Dunne. It was his profound spiritual nature that gave him the strength to get things done.

"He gave a sense of the dignity of the individual and the responsibility we have to the individual. He felt the importance of every kid. He never lost the perspective of the individual. He felt the same dignity for the most important and the least important," said Father Dunne.

"I think he first felt this when he worked with the older down and outers at the hotel (the Workingmen's Hotel, established several years before Boys Town). The older men had lost their sense of worth, esteem. He felt he wanted to preserve that early in life. I wouldn't be surprised if this wasn't what started his youth work," he explained.

"I never saw this before in someone. You sensed the greatness and the graciousness … I'm sure it communicated itself to others. He made them feel that way, too."

Father Dunne said he was not surprised by a letter received from Japan a few days after Father Flanagan's death. An Osaka woman had been honored by the Japanese press for her work with more than twenty children of lepers. She said she had been inspired during a meeting with Father Flanagan in his Oriental trip more than a year before.

"The deep impression which I received from Father Flanagan is still fresh in my mind … It will remain in my heart for good," she said.

She said she was bringing up one of the children as her own and "I am always offering prayers for the baby, that it will become a good man of God like Father Flanagan."

CHAPTER FIFTEEN

FATHER FLANAGAN TIMELINE

JULY 13, 1886	Edward Joseph Flanagan is born on Leabeg farm, near Ballymoe, Roscommon County, Ireland.
LATE SUMMER, 1904	Sails with brother P.A. Flanagan to America aboard the *S.S. Celtic*, White Star Line.
DECEMBER, 1906	**Suffers from double pneumonia and is sent home from St. Joseph's Seminary in New York the following May.**
OCTOBER, 1907	Enters Gregorian University in Rome under the auspices of the Bishop of Omaha.
JANUARY, 1908	Is sent home due to recurrence of respiratory illness.
OCTOBER 5, 1909	Enrolls in the University of Innsbruck, Austria, to study theology.
JULY 26, 1912	Is ordained a priest in Innsbruck.
1912 – 1917	Serves in several Nebraska parishes in O'Neill and Omaha.

JANUARY, 1916	Opens Workingmen's Hotel in downtown Omaha to serve homeless and jobless men.
DECEMBER 12, 1917	With a borrowed $90, rents a home at 25th and Dodge Streets and officially opens Father Flanagan's Boys' Home to five young boys assigned to him by the court.
FEBRUARY 3, 1918	Prints first issue of *Father Flanagan's Boys' Home Journal.*
JUNE 1, 1918	Moves the home to the abandoned German-American home on 13th Street.
MARCH 29, 1921	Sends his first letter appealing for funds to support the Home to Catholic residents in eastern Nebraska and western Iowa.
MAY 18, 1921	Purchases Overlook Farm, ten miles west of Omaha, as future site of the Home.
OCTOBER 22, 1921	Completes the Home's move to Overlook Farm.
JANUARY, 1926	Begins weekly radio show with the Boys' Home Band on Mondays at 6 p.m. on WAOW.
FEBRUARY 14, 1926	Institutes first student government at the Home. Boys elect first mayor and vote to officially change the name of Overlook Farm to Boys Town.
FEBRUARY, 1930	Organizes a Peace Conference at Boys Town to discuss the rights of homeless children around the world. A declaration from the conference is sent to the League of Nations.

AUGUST, 1936 | Incorporates Boys Town as a village of the state of Nebraska.

MARCH, 1938 | Meets with J. Walter Ruben and Dore Schary of MGM to review *Boys Town* movie script.

JUNE 26, 1938 | Welcomes the cast and crew of *Boys Town* to campus for ten days of location shooting.

APRIL 7, 1947 | At the invitation of the War Department, tours Japan and Korea to investigate the need for aid to war orphans and meets with Gen. Douglas MacArthur.

JULY 11, 1947 | Reports the findings of his Asian trip to President Harry S. Truman at the White House.

MARCH 11, 1948 | Arrives in Vienna, at President Truman's request, to begin looking into the plight of children orphaned in the war in Austria and Germany.

MAY 15, 1948 | Suffers a heart attack and dies in Berlin, Germany.

MAY 21, 1948 | Following two funeral Masses on campus, his body is entombed at Boys Town.

JUNE 5, 1948 | President Truman visits Boys Town and lays a wreath on Father Flanagan's tomb.

JULY 14, 1986 | U.S. Postal Service holds the first day of issue ceremony for its new four-cent Father Flanagan stamp at Boys Town, 100 years after Flanagan's birth in Ireland.